The Eldamar Cookbook

Fine Vegan Cuisine

Marian Frances White

Mary Jane's

In March of 1971 Mary Jane Payne turned the key of her first establishment and unlocked the legacy of St. John's first and, now, largest specialty food store. While Mary Jane has moved on to Hawaii where she is doing massage therapy, the little store she left behind has become a unique multi-facetted enterprise.

Mary Jane's business approach has always been innovative & community minded. We stay abreast of environmental issues and strive to implement these concerns in our products, promotion and general business operation.

Although our inventory has been augmented to encompass everything from the essential to the weird and wonderful, our primary emphasis has always been natural, healthy foods. Since Mary Jane's has been in operation we have seen a tremendous widening in our customer base, which reflects the increased knowledge and awareness of the general public. Our customers include people from various cultural & ethnic backgrounds encompassing a wide range of specialty food requirements. In addition to this, we cater to value conscious shoppers, people with special food requirements and, of course, our loyal "health food nuts" who have been with us since the beginning.

Through our book and video library, our newsletter and our lunch counter which is open daily, we endeavour to make information concerning food products, nutrition, alternative diets and therapies readily available to our customers. In this light it is our pleasure to sponsor *The Eldamar Cookbook* by Marian Frances White. Her recipes will provide a delectable sampling of the world of health food delights.

Joan Dewling,
President

377 DUCKWORTH ST.A1C 5W2 ST. JOHN'S NFLD
▫ PO BOX 5386 ▫

NATURAL FOREIGN & SPECIALTY FOODS

The Eldamar Cookbook

Fine Vegan Cuisine

Marian Frances White

Creative Publishers
St. John's, Newfoundland
1995

Acknowledgements

Without the financial contribution of Mary Jane's Ltd. this book could not have happened. Special thanks to my mother, Florence White, who taught me to bake bread and to my sisters, Ann Doran and Angela Slaney who helped me prepare the food for the photographs. Ned Pratt, a superb photographer, made a hectic weekend pleasurable. Thanks to Amy Slaney and Jackie Connors for helping with inputing recipes onto the computer. Over the years that I have been cooking vegetarian meals, I have learned a great deal from three people: my sister, (M.) White, Greg Malone and Sandy Morris. Thank you. Also, thank you to my many friends who have shared these recipes with me (especially Joy Maddigan and her family), and to the following people who contributed to or created recipes that bear their names: Elly Danica, Eileen Maxwell, Steve Power, Joan Doyle, Amelia Doran White, Ann Doran White, Connie Crane White, Dashiel and Django Morris Malone, Greg Malone, Sandy Morris, (M.Naeme) White, Margaret Atwood, Twyla Weixl and Lorraine Desjardins. Special appreciation to Beni Malone and our daughter, Anahareo, for inspiring so many of these recipes (and for cleaning up after a flurry of guests had left). Lastly, thank you to Don Morgan at Creative Book Publishing for believing in The Eldamar Cookbook.

Cover and other photographs (except where otherwise identifed) are by Ned Pratt

∝ Printed on re-cycled, acid-free paper

Published by
CREATIVE BOOK PUBLISHING
A Division of 10699 Newfoundland Limited
A Robinson-Blackmore Printing & Publishing associated company
P.O. Box 8660, St. John's, Newfoundland A1B 3T7

Printed in Canada by:
ROBINSON-BLACKMORE PRINTING & PUBLISHING

Canadian Cataloguing in Publication Data
White, Marian Frances, 1954–
    The Eldamar cookbook

    Includes index.
    ISBN 1-895387-61-2

1. Vegetarian cookery.   I. Title

TX837.W54   1995   641.5'636   C95-950315-3

Dedicated to Tommy Sexton
(1957-1993)
who enjoyed many vegan meals
at my home
and
to my daughter
Anahareo
who enjoyed them with him

Table of Contents

Acknowledgements _____ iv

Foreword _____ ix

Introduction _____ xi

Soups, Salads and Dressings _____ 1

Breads, Pastries and Pancakes _____ 17

Main Dishes with Trimmings _____ 35

Desserts _____ 63

Glossary _____ 81

Index _____ 82

Foreword

One Sunday morning when our children were still babies my family trooped over to Marian's apartment in St. John's to enjoy a brunch of Marian's plump chocolate covered whole wheat donuts. They were laid out piping hot on the kitchen table and the sweet aroma filled the house.

After the donuts had cooled a little I went in to sample one. There wasn't one there. I asked Marian where she had put them. No where. This began a frantic search for the donuts that we had already mentally digested. No, the table was clean as a whistle and the cupboards and the floor.

However in the corner was our Gordon Setter, Rosie, looking up at us with a look on her dog's face that could only be described as *sheepish*. With a guilty side long glance she slunk out of the room. On one whisker was a crumb of donut with the barest trace of chocolate, the only physical remains of two dozen chocolate donuts. We were shocked. It seemed impossible and improbable that Rosie could have eaten every last one without a trace. But as Sherlock Holmes said, when the improbable is the only explanation left, then it is the answer.

If we didn't already know we were reminded then of the irresistible and universal appeal of Marian's baking.

We all came to the vegan diet as big food enthusiasts and avid cooks. With the vegan diet the food for us kept getting better and better. It isn't substitute food, it is the first food — Nature's best — and guests at Marian's dinner table do not feel the lack or absence of anything. It's wonderful to eat the tastiest of lentil soups and know that not only does it not have cholesterol, but that the lentils actually reduce cholesterol in the body. Many families in this northern climate have grown and flourished on the vegan recipes in this book.

Rosie knew all of this and that dog lived to be almost seventeen, quite a ripe old age for a setter. But really, to be honest, I must admit that the dog ate those two dozen donuts just for the taste.

So enjoy these recipes for the taste. And if you find yourself slim and healthy at seventy-five, you can blame it on the donuts.

—Greg Malone

Introduction

When I am outside the city in Newfoundland, I feel that I have entered a fairyland. The Avalon Peninsula alone offers enough delights for a lifetime. Eldamar is the fairy name for a magical place you call home. I found this place in Avondale where berries grow in abundance and wild rose bushes lead you to a chanterelle mushroom forest. Eldamar can be found whenever you enter that soul place — a place where food tastes like an elixir of life and where it can truly be said that the earth has been blessed. It was in Eldamar, my country home in Avondale, that I concocted many of these recipes.

The idea for *The Eldamar Cookbook* came from my friends — a long overdue promise to share culinary delights. Ever since I became a strict vegetarian in the mid 70s, I have attempted to concoct meals that are both satisfying nutritionally, as well as pleasing to the palate. During this time I have also been fortunate to have eaten many pleasing dinners and desserts prepared by other people. Some of these are contained in the following pages.

My first cooking experiences (outside of my parents' kitchen) were as a teenager in the Carleton University cafeteria, Ottawa. There I subsidized my journalism fees by cooking huge amounts of food for the students who lived in the residents at Carleton. It was in Ottawa that I met my first live/healthy vegetarian, Twyla Dawn Weixl. Later when my curiosity took me west, I subsidized my meagre writing earnings with a part-time job as a chef at a youth hostel in Vancouver. There I had to conceal my vegetarianism in order to get and maintain the job. Years later while spending several months in Jamaica, I absorbed the wise words of the Rastafarian philosopher, Maurice, as he conjured up Ital Soup and spoke of the connections between islands, especially Newfoundland and Jamaica.

Sometimes when I am preparing food in my kitchen I feel I am carrying out some feminist, political act. It is there I can take control of my own health and to a degree avoid the costly and often harrowing experiences of institutionalized health care.

My biggest challenge in compiling this cookbook has been having to be precise about my recipes. I am known to add a pinch of this and a dab of that at the last minute. I am also known to revise recipes that were seemingly perfect. So, I encourage you to experiment with these recipes and adjust the ingredients to suit your own taste. More recently, I have attempted to experiment with wheatfree flour and pasta. For those of you with food allergies, try substituting pea, corn, rice or millet flour in any of the dishes.

The recipes contained here were born out of necessity. When I became a vegetarian there were few recipe books to consult, and obtaining special ingredients was no easy task. Mary Jane's has always been a refuge for me. Being a strict vegetarian in the mid seventies was not nearly as socially acceptable as it is today. There were many awkward moments as I explained that I not only did not eat meat, I also did not eat fish, eggs, or any form of dairy products. Few believed I could survive, let alone thrive. I read whatever I could find on vegetarianism and later enrolled at Hippocrates Health Institute in Boston. There I spent several months studying this alternative lifestyle. Besides not eating from the animal kingdom, I began a wholistic approach to my life, doing yoga, studying herbs and familiarizing myself with the new concept of being relaxed and in touch with my body.

There was no fridge or stove in our kitchen at Hippocrates. All the food was prepared and served in its raw state; this was called "live food." (Raw food has a high enzyme content—the life principle in all living things.) I studied there under some of the world's most renowned health professionals; Dr. Ann Wigmore and Viktoras Kulvinskas. There were guest lecturers and conferences lead by the herbalist Dr. John Christopher. The Macrobiotic School under the direction of Michio Kushi, was a mere two blocks down Newbury St. Although I went there for lectures, I always felt a bit sacrilegious, not unlike a Catholic going to a Protestant service — they cooked their food and even ate animal products occasionally! What I gained from Mr. Kushi's lectures was knowledge of the eastern concepts of yin and yang and polarity balancing. There I digested Dr. Randolf Stone's essential truth — if you are happy you can digest a rock!

While I continue to carry with me many of the basic truths I first discovered at Hippocrates, over the years I have grown to accept a vegetarian diet for a northern climate; one that is a combination of raw fruits, sprouts, nuts and vegetables, as well as a wide variety of cooked foods that include grains, pastas and legumes. However, I feel the healthiest diet is one that consists of at least 50% raw foods.

In the glossary at the back of this book, I define several products that might not be familiar to the aspiring vegetarian or adventurous cook. If you come across some unusual food or reference in the recipes, chances are you will find an explanation in the glossary. I suggest you consult this glossary before trying the recipes.

Health be yours, as you enjoy the rewards of vegetarian dining!

—Marian Frances White

Soups,
Salads
and
Dressings

Soups

About Soups _____ 3

Miso Bean Soup _____ 3

Lima Bean Soup _____ 3

Zucchini Soupe de Sand _____ 4

Split Pea Soup _____ 4

Lentil Soup_____ 4

Gazpacho Soup _____ 5

Minestrone Soup_____ 5

Borsch _____ 5

Beet Soup for the Fall _____ 6

Soup à l'Oignon (French Onion Soup)_____ 6

Full Moon Corn Chowder _____ 7

Tofu Soup For Two _____ 7

I-tal Soup_____ 7

Salads

Falling Into The Bowl Fruit Salad _____ 9

Chlorophyll Garden Salad _____ 9

Caesar Salad _____ 9

Healing Cole Slaw _____ 10

Sprout Salads _____ 10

Half Moon Bean Salad_____ 11

Summer Potato Salad _____ 11

Newfanese Potato Salad _____ 11

Salad Dressings and Sauces

Soyanaise _____ 12

Anahareo's Fave-Tahini Dressing _____ 12

Colour Therapy Dressing _____ 12

Tossed Salad Dressing_____ 13

Showy Tofu Dressing _____ 13

Parsley Garlic Dressing _____ 13

Pesto _____ 13

Hippocrates Rejuvelac _____ 14

Boston Seed Yogurt _____ 14

A Winter's Breakfast_____ 15

Southern Bell Guacamole _____ 15

Soups

About Soups

As with steaming vegetables rather than boiling them (iodine is lost in the cooking water), don't destroy the life of your soup by boiling or over cooking it.

If you are adding grains or pasta, cook them separate before adding to vegetables. To avoid gas from beans, discard the water that you soak the beans in, or use it (diluted) to water your house plants.

Use the steaming water from vegetables for your soup stock.

Miso Bean Soup

Soak and cook until soft

1 cup	mixed bean soup mix in 6 cups of water

Add:

2 tbsp.	brown rice miso
1	large diced onion
1	small diced green pepper
3	potatoes chopped small
2	medium carrots chopped small
1 cup	diced turnip

Herbs:

1 tsp.	each of thyme and parsley
1 tbsp.	Bernard Jensen Broth and Seasoning
1 tsp.	Protein Seasoning

Simmer, stir occasionally until vegetables are tender, but never over done, approximately 30 minutes

Serve with sesame crackers & lecithin spread

Lima Bean Soup

Soak 1 cup lima beans for 2 hours

Cook until soft (approximately 1 hour)

Add:

1	med. diced onion
1	stalk celery, finely diced
2	med. potatoes diced
1 cup	diced carrot
1 tsp.	oregano & thyme combined
2 tbsp.	miso paste

Simmer until vegetables are tender.

Do not over cook.

Before serving add 2 tbsp. liquid mineral bouillon.

Zucchini Soupe de Sand

Blend 3 medium onions with 1/4 cup oil

Fry 1/4 cup olive oil with

1 tbsp.	protein seasoning
2	cloves garlic
1 tsp.	cumin

Add blended onions and continue frying until golden

Add

1/4 cup	chick pea flour and
2 cups	vegie stock (1 tbsp. Bernard Jensen Seasoning and 1 tbsp. Protein Seasoning) enough to make consistency of gravy.

Blend

2	medium zucchini until smooth and pour into stock pot

Simmer for 15 minutes

Serve with a dollop of *Pesto* and a sprinkling of fresh dill

This soup is also delicious made from cucumber.

Split Pea Soup

Cook until tender:

1 cup yellow split peas	
	in
6 cups	water
	and
1	bay leaf

Add:

1 tbsp.	miso paste
1 cup	chopped onion
1 cup	chopped celery with leaves
1 cup	diced carrot and turnip
2 cups	diced potato

Cook until tender and season with black pepper, a pinch of thyme and a little sea salt.

Lentil Soup

Bring to a boil 1 cup washed lentils in 12 cups of vegetable broth.
Simmer for 1 hour over medium heat.

Add:

1 cup	chopped onion
1	bay leaf
1 tsp.	tumeric
1 tbsp.	Protein Seasoning

Blend and add:

1	medium carrot
4	medium potatoes
2 cups	stewed tomatoes

Serve with hot soup rolls.

Gazpacho – a cold and tasty soup

Blend:

1 clove	garlic
1 cup	onion
3 lbs.	tomatoes
2	medium cucumber
1	green pepper
2 cups	tomato juice
1/3 cup	olive oil
3 tbsp.	apple cider vinegar
2 tsp.	Protein Seasoning
2 tsp.	paprika
	dash of pepper and sea salt

Chill thoroughly before serving.

Minestrone

6 cups	vegetable broth
1 clove	diced garlic
1 cup	chopped onion
1 cup	minced celery
1/4 cup	parsley
1/4 tsp.	oregano
1/8 tsp.	cayenne pepper
1 tsp.	Protein Seasoning
3 cups	tomatoes (Cut in quarters)
1 cup	grated cabbage
1 cup	cooked and drained chick peas
1 cup	macaroni of your choice

Simmer all ingredients in a saucepan for half an hour.

Borsch For Twyla Dawn Weixl

4 cups	shredded raw beet
3 cups	shredded raw cabbage
1 cup	diced onion
1 cup	celery
6 cups	vegetable broth

| 2 tsp. | Protein Seasoning |

Place ingredients in a pot and cook (covered) on a meduim heat for half an hour.

Add 1 tbsp. lemon juice before serving

Beet Soup for the Fall

| 1 cup | navy beans, soak & cook until soft in |
| 4 cups | water (for 2 hours) |

Drain and add:

2	grated beets
2	grated carrots
1/2	med. grated cabbage
2	grated onions
4 cups	hot water

Let simmer until vegetables are tender

While simmering add:

1 tbsp.	Fresh cut oregano and parsley
3 tbsp.	brown rice miso
1 tbsp.	Bernard Jensen's Broth and Seasoning.

Soupe à l'Oignon (French Onion Soup)

6	medium onions
2 cloves	garlic
2 tbsp.	olive oil
1 cup	croutons
1 cup	soy cheese (grated optional)
1/4 cup	miso paste
2 tbsp.	corn or yellow pea flour
1/4 tsp.	thyme
2 tsp.	Protein Seasoning
4 cups	water

Use a cast iron pot or deep frying pan.

Cut onions in thin circles and fry with minced garlic until golden but not brown. Add the flour and stir until oil is absorbed. Add a little water at a time (to prevent lumpiness). Next stir in miso until it has dissolved. Simmer for 20 minutes. Consistency should not be thick, but somewhat creamy.

Pour equal amounts into oven proof bowls, top with croutons and grated soy cheese (optional). Broil until soy cheese is golden brown. To make croutons see *Caesar Salad*, pg. 9.)

Serve tout de suite!

Full Moon Corn Chowder

Bring 3 cups water to boil while chopping 3 med. potatoes (or grating fine in a food processor, if you prefer a smoother chowder)

Add to pot:

1 cup	onion finely cut
2 cups	grated corn
1 cup	med carrot
1 tsp.	savoury, celery seed and dill combined
1 tbsp.	Protein Seasoning.

Simmer for 30 min. with 1 tsp. miso paste

Towards end of cooking pour in 1 cup soy or almond milk.

Heat but do not boil.

Serve with a dollop of *Pesto*.

Tofu Soup For Two

Simmer these ingredients until tender:

1 cup	cooked basmati rice in
6 cups	spring water
2	diced carrot
3	diced potato
1/2 cup	celery
1/2 cup	peas
1 cup	diced onion
1 lb.	tofu, cut in tiny cubes

Season with a combination of:

1 tsp.	tarragon, basil and oregano
1 tsp.	mineral bouillon
1 tsp.	Protein Seasoning
1 tsp.	miso paste

I-tal Soup

A Jamaican dish eaten almost daily by Rastafarian followers. Revised for a northern climate and stock on hand.

Where possible use a fresh coconut.*

Crack and grate the coconut.

Soak the pulp for half an hour in 2 cups of hot water (retain water). Squeeze pulp through a cheese cloth to make a pure and delicious (Irie as the Rastas say) coconut milk. This is the base of the soup—its stock.

If you have a sturdy juicer you can also make the juice by following the above directions, however instead of grating, you put the small pieces through the juicer to make a delicious coconut cream.

In a stewing pot pour the stock and the retained water.

Add the following chopped vegetables:

1/2 cup	onion
1/2 cup	green or red pepper
1 cup	sweet potato
1 cup	potato
2 cups	chopped spinach or turnip tops
2 cups	spring water for a thinner base.

Simmer for 1/4 hour on a medium heat.

Add 1/4 tsp. of each of the following herbs: savoury, thyme, and parsley.

Before serving sprinkle on:

1 tsp.	cayenne,
1 tbsp.	Bernard Jensen's Broth or Seasoning
1 tbsp.	Protein Seasoning.

*If a fresh coconut is not available use dried creamed coconut or soak diced coconut overnight in warm water.

"The Eldamar Garden"

Falling Into The Bowl Fruit Salad

Dice the folowing:

3	red delicious apples
1	large, ripe banana
2 tsp.	lemon juice
1/2 cup raisins (soaked the night before)	
1	cubed orange
	juice of 1 orange

Garnish with red seedless grapes

Suggested topping: Serve with fresh coconut cream(see page 7).

Chlorophyll Garden Salad

Clean and prepare 1 head of Boston crisp lettuce or other crisp leaf lettuce

Finely cut in the following fresh herbs:

Chives Basil Garlic and Thyme

Add 1 finely grated carrot

2 quartered vine ripened tomatoes

Serve with *Tossed Salad Dressing* (pg. 13).

Caesar Salad

Have ready:

1	large romaine lettuce washed and drained. Tear into pieces and put in a salad bowl
1/2 cup	croutons (easily made from not so fresh bread, cut in tiny 1/2 inch cubes and spread along a baking sheet. Sprikle a few tablespoons of olive oil over this and bake at 300° for 30 minutes. Two slices of bread equals 1 cup of croutons.)

In a measuring cup combine the following:

2 tsp.	lemon juice
1/4 cup	olive oil
1 tsp.	Protein Seasoning
1 clove	crushed garlic
1/2 cup	soy Parmesan cheese
1/4	cup *Soyanaise* (page 12)

Toss these mixed seasonings throughout the lettuce and then add croutons.

Healing Cole Slaw

1	small cabbage sliced in quarters (take off outer leaves and use in cabbage rolls)
1/4 cup	fresh lemon juice (or more if you like a tarter taste)
2 tsp.	Protein Seasoning
4 cloves	garlic (minced)
1/4 cup	olive oil
1	med carrot

Grate cabbage to a pulp by hand or in a Food Processor
Add remaining ingredients. Do not over blend. Serve fresh.

Sprout Salads

All unhulled seeds, like alfalfa, mung beans and even lentils can be sprouted. Sprouted beans and grains are complete proteins. When these foods are germinating they produce proteins, vitamins, and minerals. Sprouts are an inexpensive food source. They are easy to grow at home and give a constant source of fresh, nutritious food all year round. Try sprouts in salads, on sandwiches, or on their own.

To sprout any seed soak over night in a large mason jar or other large jar (example: 1/4 cup of alfalfa seed to 2 cups of water)

Place a thin wire mesh over the mouth of the jar and drain off the excess water. (This water can be diluted to use in watering house plants.)

Rinse the seeds thoroughly by allowing water to run over the brim of the bottle. Turn over and drain. Keep jar in the reverse position while sprouting. Cover the jar with a cloth and rinse twice daily. In 1 week your jar will be full of sprouts.

But first they must be cleaned and then put in the light to gain chlorophyll.

Cleaning method: Pour the entire contents of the jar directly into a stainless steel sink or large stainless steel bowl. Clean jar thoroughly. As you put the sprouted seeds into the water, the hulls or tops of the seeds will rise to the top (or most of them will). Pull these hulls to one side and take the sprouts from the water, returning to the clean jar. Cover once again with mesh, turn upside down to drain excess water and place in sunny location. Rinse once a day. Within two days the tips of the sprout will turn green.

They are now ready to serve in a salad or on sandwiches.

To keep sprouts fresh keep in refrigerator or in a very cool room.

Please note, mung beans and other large beans do not like to be kept in the light. They are ready to eat once they have sprouted.

Half Moon Bean Salad

1 1/2 cups	cooked kidney beans
1 cup	cooked and well drained chick peas
1 cup	green string beans, cut in 1" pieces
1/2 cup	finely chopped celery
1/2 cup	onion half moons

Combine in a salad bowl and toss lightly with a little oil, apple cidar vinegar, a tsp. of Protein Seasoning and a pinch of black pepper.

Summer Potato Salad

Prepare:

| 8 or 10 | new potatoes, cooked and cubed with skins |
| 2 beets | cooked and cubed |

Sauté

1/2 lb.	sliced mushrooms, with 1 medium onion
2 whole	cucumbers, peeled and cubed (thin)
1/2 cup	parsley, chopped
2/3 cup	olive oil
1/3 cup	apple cider vinegar
1 tbsp.	french mustard

Season to taste with: pepper, Bernard Jensen's Broth and Seasonig and Protein Seasoning

Toss together in a bowl and serve chilled

Newfanese Potato Salad

Steam 10 medium potatoes and 1 large carrot, finely cut

1	medium onion diced
1 cup	fresh or frozen peas
1 cup	*Soyanaise*

Method: In a mixing bowl, mash potatoes when hot and then add the diced onion, finely chopped carrot and peas that have been lightly cooked and allowed to cool.

Mix in soyanaise and add:

    1 tsp. Bernard Jensen's

    2 tsp. Protein Seasoning.

Smooth the top of the salad and sprinkle top with paprika.

Cool before serving.

Soyanaise

Pour into a food processor or blender

1 cup	soy milk

While blending add

1 cup	sunflower oil (or other oil of your choice)

Continue adding up to one more cup of oil until mixture begins to thicken, not unlike regular mayonnaise.

Season with a tbsp. of lemon juice and a pinch of sea salt or Protein Seasoning. Protein Seasoning will darken the soyanaise.

Options: Dress with dill and parsley, or use plain and simple.

Bottle and chill for immediate use.

Anahareo's Fave Tahini Dressing

2 tbsp.	tahini
3/4 cup	sunflower oil
2 tbsp.	apple cider vinegar
2 tbsp.	spring water
1 tbsp.	mustard

Hand blend until smooth

Add:

2 cloves	pressed garlic
1 tsp.	Protein Seasoning
1/2 tsp.	parsley
1/2 tsp.	Bernard Jensen Broth or Seasoning

If too thick add more vinegar (if you want a sharper taste) or oil for a smooth consistency.

Colour Therapy Salad Dressing

Blend smooth for a thick dressing:

1/2 lb.	soft tofu
1/2 cup	pure water
3/4 cup	olive oil
1/2 cup	onion
1/4 cup	beet juice (pickled)
	or
1/4 cup	grated beet and juice of 1 lemon
1 tsp.	dill
1 tsp.	basil
1 tbsp.	Protein Seasoning
1/2 tsp.	horseradish powder or mustard

Tossed Salad Dressing

With salad in bowl and herbs finely cut in (fresh basil, parsley, thyme, and dill)

Toss in

1/2 cup	olive oil

Sprinkle on

1/4 cup	nutritional yeast flakes
1 tbsp.	Bernard Jensen's broth and seasoning
1 tsp.	Protein Seasoning (optional)

Pour juice of 1 lemon over this or 2 tbsp. apple cider vinegar

Toss again and serve

Showy Tofu Dressing

Blend:

8 oz	soft tofu with
1/4 cup	fresh lemon juice
1/4 cup	corn oil
1 tsp.	dill
1 tsp.	Bernard Jensen's Seasoning
2 tsp.	parsley

Parsley Garlic Dressing

1 cup	olive oil
1/4 cup	fresh lemon juice
1 cup	parsley (fresh)
4 cloves	garlic pressed
1 tsp.	Protein Seasoning
1 tbsp.	nutritional yeast (optional)

Blend till smooth

Pesto

In a Food Processor or blender combine the following:

1 lb.	fresh basil leaves
6 cloves	garlic
2 cups	olive oil
1 tbsp.	Protein Seasoning

Blend until smooth and creamy.

Optional: Add 1/2 cup pine nuts. I rarely use nuts in making pesto since they go rancid easily and can ruin your precious pesto, but this is a delightful addition if you are serving the pesto immediately.

Store in small, sterilized mason jars. These can be frozen and used at your leisure.

Pesto is especially delicious served over any pasta dish.

Hippocrates Rejuvelac

This is a fermented grain liquid that is used as the fermenting agent in making yogurt. Use soft wheat berries. Rejuvelac is high in B vitamins and also has vitamin C. Wash berries well.

In a mason jar combine:

1/2 cup	wheat berries
3 cups	water

Cover loosely with the lid.

Be sure to also cover jar with a cloth.

Soak in this water for 48 hours.

Keep the liquid at room temperature.

When water has a sweet fermented smell, not sour, pour liquid off and use as rejuvelac.

Add 2 more cups of water to berries and let soak again for 24 hours — pour off liquid and you have more rejuvelac. This is the peak day for the highest vitamin and enzyme content. Rejuvelac gets strong tasting after 2nd and 3rd day. A word of caution — fermented foods should be used with reservation by persons with overacid stomachs.

Use this rejuvelac in *Boston Seed Yogurt.*

Boston Seed Yogurt

(A Fermented Seed Sauce I learned from Dr. Ann Wigmore)

2 cups	ground hulled sunflower seeds
1 cup	ground almonds

Grind in a coffee grinder or hand food grinder.

Combine seeds and add enough rejuvelac to make the consistency of pancake batter.

Now you have a smooth creamy sauce that you can pour into either a glass or a stainless steel container (Please no aluminum or plastic —the fermentation taking place will stir up the molecules in aluminum and plastic containers, which end up depositing themselves in our bodies).

Cover loosely (a plate or bowl on top will do).

Set in a warm place for 6 to 8 hours. Ideal temperature is 70 to 100°. I use an electric yogurt maker, although a covered glass jar in the sun or on a hot water radiator works just as well.

When the sauce is fermented the "whey" will sink to the bottom of the container. Stir the "whey" in to the yogurt because it contains valuable enzymes and vitamins.

Chill before serving. Delicious with *A Winter's Breakfast.*

A Winter's Breakfast

Soak in spring water overnight:

4 or 6	organic apricots
1/2 cup	organic seedless raisins

In the morning grate 2 red delicious apples in a bowl and cut in

1	banana

Serve with soaked fruit and a heaping tablespoon of *Boston Seed Yogurt*.

Eat immediately as the apples will oxidize when exposed to the air causing the fruit to discolour. Pour a little of the juice from the soaked fruit over the yogurt. Enjoy a truly comforting winter's breakfast.

Southern Bell Guacamole

1 lg.	ripe avocado or 2 small ones
	juice of 1 lime
1 to 2	cloves garlic (crushed)
1/4 cup	bell pepper (finely cut)
1 med.	diced tomato
1/4 cup	finely chopped red onion
1/2 tsp.	hotpepper sauce
1/2 tsp.	cayenne pepper
1 tsp.	Protein Seasoning

Mash and mix well, serve as an entre with corn chips.

HINTS TO MAKE FOOD PREPARING EASIER:

KITCHEN AIDS:
VEGETABLE JUICER
FOOD PROCESSOR
SEED GRINDER OR COFFEE GRINDER FOR NUTS & SEEDS
WATER DISTILLER AND/OR SPRING WATER
LARGE CUTTING BOARD
GARLIC PRESS AND DOUBLE EDGE GRATER.
ALWAYS USE GOOD QUALITY KITCHEN UTENSILS — (STAINLESS STEEL & CAST IRON).

WHEN MEASURING LIQUIDS, PLACE ON
COUNTER TOP AND READ AT EYE LEVEL.

WHEN MEASURING FLOUR, DO NOT SHAKE
MEASURING JUG WHICH SETTLES THE FLOUR.

HERE ARE SOME BASIC FOOD COMBINING
SUGGESTIONS THAT I HAVE FOUND HELPFUL
IN THE ASSIMILATION AND DIGESTION OF
FOOD:

FOR EASY DIGESTION, MELONS SHOULD BE
EATEN ALONE OR LEFT ALONE.

DRIED FRUIT IS BEST SOAKED BECAUSE THE
WATER BRINGS LIFE TO THE FRUIT. SUGAR
IN THE FRUIT IS NOT AS CONCENTRATED
WHEN SOAKED.

PROTEINS (NUTS, SEEDS AND BEANS ETC.)
DO NOT COMINE WELL WITH STARCHES (PO-
TATO, CORN OR PASTA). PROTEIN FOODS
COMBINE WELL WITH GREEN AND LOW
STARCH VEGETABLES.

ACID FRUITS (ORGANGES, PINEAPPLE, LEM-
ONS ETC.) DO NOT COMBINE WELL WITH
SWEET FRUITS (BANANA, DATES OR PA-
PAYA). HOWEVER, ACID FRUITS COMBINE
WELL WITH SUB-ACID FRUITS SUCH AS APPLE,
APRICOT AND BERRIES. AS WELL, SWEET
FRUITS COMBINE FAIRLY WELL WITH SUB-
ACID FRUITS.

KITCHEN HERBS I HAVE FOUND USEFUL FOR
MEDICINAL PURPOSES:

GINGER FOR STOMACH CRAMPS AND GAS.

CLOVES FOR SORE GUMS AND TOOTHACHE.

MINT TEA FOR INDIGESTION.

YARROW TO COUNTERACT A FEVER.

SAGE AND SEA SALT GARGLE FOR A SORE
THROAT.

Breads,
Pastries
and
Pancakes

Calm-me-down Cinnamon Rolls _____ 19

Extra Terrestrial Raised Doughnuts _____ 20

Whole Wheat Protein Bread _____ 21

Dark Pumpernickel Bread _____ 22

Lassy Bread _____ 22

Connie's Banana Bread _____ 23

Solstice Parachute Ginger Bread _____ 23

Figgy Duff _____ 24

Pita Bread _____ 25

Tofu Herb Rolls _____ 25

Corn Meal Buns or Bread _____ 26

Figgie Lizzie Tea Buns _____ 26

Lightweight Bran Muffins _____ 27

Honey Scones _____ 27

Margaret Atwood Wheat Germ Muffins
    Revised and Edited_____ 28

Quidi Vidi Road Soup Biscuits _____ 28

Doyle's Zucchini Loaf _____ 29

Special Occasion Pancakes _____ 29

Magic Potion Apple Pancakes _____ 30

Scorpio Sun Celebration Pancakes_____ 30

Yesteryear Pancakes For Today's Diet _____ 31

Heavenly Crepes _____ 31

Savory Crepes _____ 31

Pie Crust That Works _____ 32

Amelia's Raspberry Turnovers _____ 32

No Tricks Pumpkin Pie _____ 32

Raspberry Tofu Pie _____ 33

From Another Time Apple Pie_____ 33

Wild Blueberry Pie_____ 34

Calm-Me-Down-Cinnamon Rolls

Yield: 2 doz.

Soak 1 cup raisins in 1 cup warm water

Dissolve 1 tbsp. honey in 1 1/2 cups warm water

Sprinkle 2 tbsp. dry active yeast into water

Let rise for at least 10 minutes

Keep temperature warm and constant until yeast is light and foamy

In a large mixing bowl measure 6 cups lightly sifted flour

Using a pastry cutter, cut in 3/4 cup corn or sunflower oil

Stir in risen yeast

Add 1/2 cup of lightly sweetened water to mixture

Sprinkle in 1 tbsp. cinnamon

Mix well and knead with your hands for ten minutes adding a sprinkling of flour to keep dough from sticking to sides of bowl

Cover with a cloth and let rise in a warm place for 30 minutes.

Meanwhile you can putter around the kitchen doing a necessary task that would otherwise never get done, for example, organize spice labels or recipe file

Preheat oven to 350°

When almost double in bulk sprinkle flour on a table or cutting board and roll dough onto it

Lightly oil the dough with an oiling brush along the surface

Spread a thin layer of honey evenly along the dough

Sprinkle lots of cinnamon over the honey

Add 1 cup soaked raisins (well-drained) and a few crushed nuts over surface (optional)

Roll dough away from you until one end meets the other

Cut in 3/4" circles and place on oiled baking sheet

Brush top of rolls with oil

Bake at 350° for one-half hour

While warm, grate coconut cream over rolls

When cool, calmly devour with friends

Extra Terrestrial Raised Doughnuts From Mars

1 cup	warm water
2 tbsp.	dry active yeast
2 tbsp.	honey or maple syrup

Dissolve honey in water; sprinkle yeast on top

Let rise till foamy (about 15 minutes)

In a Cuisine Art,Food Processor or by hand mix:

2 cups	soft whole wheat flour (or unbleached white)
1 tbsp.	cinnamon and 1 tsp. nutmeg
2 cups	warm soy milk
1/2 cup	honey or maple syrup
1/2 cup	sunflower or other unrefined light oil
2 tbsp.	liquid lecithin
1 tsp.	sea salt

Pour in risen yeast and mix for 2 minutes

Gradually add 4 cups flour to blended mixture until a light dough is formed. Continue to blend for 5 minues.

In a large mixing bowl add 2 cups four and pour in dough from food processor. Stir until you have a very stiff dough. Add up to 2 more cups of flour and begin to knead.

Knead in bowl or turn dough onto board adding more flour if dough is too sticky. Knead until you see stars (at least 10 minutes). Dough should be light and bounce back when pressed.

Lightly oil dough, place in oiled bowl, cover with a clean cloth and an additional cover for extra warmth.

Let rise in a warm place until double in bulk.

Turn dough onto lightly floured board and roll out with a rolling pin to 1/2 in. thickness.

Cut with doughnut cutter and let individual doughnuts rise on floured board.

Meanwhile heat 4 cups unprocessed light oil (sunflower or corn) in deep fryer to 375°. Test one doughnut for ideal frying temperature. Doughnut should rise to the top soon after it is placed in the oil.

Doughnuts fry quickly, 1 1/2 to 2 minutes on each side is plenty.

To prevent pricking the surface, use thongs to remove doughnuts from oil.

Lay on brown paper to drain off excess oil.

Cool before glazing.

Glaze for Doughnuts

1 cup	carob or melted dark chocolate
1/2 cup	honey

Stir till creamy

Add 1 tsp. oil

Dip surface of doughnut into glaze

Hint: Beware of Dogs lurking under your kitchen table!(See pg. ix)

The Eldamar Cookbook

Whole Wheat Protein Bread

Dissolve 1 tbsp. honey in 1 1/2 cups warm water

Sprinkle 3 tbsp. dry active yeast on top

Stir lightly. Let sit until light and foamy (about 10 minutes)

Meanwhile heat 32 oz of water, do not boil

Prepare the following in a large bread bowl:

4 lbs.	whole wheat flour
1/2 cup	soy flour, alfalfa or rice flour

Stir in

1 tbsp.	protein seasoning or kelp powder

Pour warm water into another bowl

Add

1/2 cup	sunflower oil or other light oil
1/2 cup	honey or blackstrap molasses if a darker bread is desired
1 tbsp.	liquid lecithin. Mix together.

Kneading:

This kneading method I learnt from my mother Florence White.

Prepare the flour in a large bowl and form a volcano-like hole with your hand.

Pour risen yeast in the centre and then add the other wet ingredients.

Stir with a wooden spoon until it gets very stiff.

Now it's time to start kneading with your hands. This is done by turning and folding the dough, gradually sprinkling flour on the bottom of the bowl to prevent the dough from sticking. Continue this process for 10 minutes either retain dough in the pan, or turn onto a well-floured board or table for kneading.

Put dough aside; clean bowl, lightly oil the inside and return dough to the bowl.

Flip dough over and cover with a clean cloth to keep dough warm while rising to double in bulk. This will take approximately 2 hrs.

Knead down for several minutes and allow to rise again until double in bulk. This second rising should take 1 hr.

Preheat oven to 325°

After a second rising, cut off a large slice of dough and form loaves by smoothing and shaping the dough. Make 2 or 3 mounds for each bread pan.

Place in lightly oiled bread pans — stainless steel, glass or cast iron preferably.

Cover and let rise in pans until they have once again doubled in bulk.

Bake for 50 minutes until golden brown

Remove from pans and place on cooling rack.

If you prefer a soft crust, brush a small amount of oil along top.

(Note: Sour dough bread can be made by letting the regular bread rise too long, kneading and letting rise again. Try cutting off a cup of dough and cover with water. Keep in fridge until ready to use as you would yeast.)

Dark Pumpernickel Bread

Dissolve 2 tbsp. dry active yeast in:

    1 1/2 cups   warm, honey sweetened water and let rise for 15 minutes.

Mix the following in a large bowl:

1 tbsp.	protein seasoning or other salt substitute
2 tsp.	caraway seeds
3 cups	rye flour
1/4 cup	carob
2 1/2 cups	whole wheat flour
2 tbsp.	oil or tahini
1 cup	warm soy milk

Combine risen yeast with the above ingredients.

Mix well till dough falls away from side of pan.

Turn onto a floured board to knead (10 minutes).

Place in lightly oiled bowl and let rise covered for 1 hour.

Punch down; let rise 40 minutes more.

Sprinkle baking sheet with cornmeal.

Shape each loaf into a mound on opposite corners of sheet.

Let rise one more hour in warm environment.

Preheat oven to 350° and bake for 30 – 35 minutes.

When loaves sound hollow they are baked.

Lassy Bread

Makes 2 loaves.

1 tsp.	raw sugar
1/2 cup	warm water
1 tbsp.	dry active yeast
2 1/2 cups	soy milk
1/4 cup	corn oil
1 tbsp.	sea salt
1/2 cup	molasses
6–7 cups	light flour
2 tsp.	cinnamon
1 tsp.	mace
1 tsp.	cloves
2 cups	raisins

Dissolve yeast in lukewarm water to which 1 tsp. raw sugar has been added.

Leave undisturbed for 10-15 minutes until yeast is bubbly.

In a saucepan, warm milk, oil and sea salt.

In large mixing bowl, combine molasses, yeast mixture and 3 cups flour and spices. Beat with wooden spoon 2-3 minutes. Continue adding flour until moist soft dough is formed. Add raisins.

Place on floured table or board and knead for about 10 minutes until dough becomes smooth and elastic (add more flour if dough is sticky).

Cover with a cloth.

Place in lightly oiled bowl and in a warm place until double in bulk (1 1/2 – 2 hours).

Divide dough in half and shape to form 2 loaves, making the surface smooth.

Place in 2 oiled 5" X 9" loaf pans and allow to rise again until doubled (1–2 hours). Loosely cover pans with a clean, damp cup towel.

Preheat oven to 325°.

Bake until loaves are brown and give a hollow sound when tapped (about 1 hour). Brush tops with oil while hot.

Connie's Banana Bread

Preheat oven to 350°.

Use Cuisine Art or Food Processor to combine:

1/2 cup	soy milk
1/4 cup	light oil
3/4 cup	honey
1 tsp.	grated orange rind
1 3/4 cup	light flour
1 tsp.	baking powder
1 tsp.	baking soda
Pinch	salt substitute

Mash and add 3 ripe bananas.

Do not over blend.

Pour into oiled bread pan.

Bake for 45 – 50 minutes.

Let stand for a few minutes and then remove from pan to cool.

Solstice Parachute Ginger Bread

2 cups	light flour (your combination)
1 tsp.	baking powder
1 tsp.	baking soda
1 cup	mild flavoured molasses
1/2 cup	light oil
2 tsp.	ginger
1/2 tsp.	salt substitute or sea salt
1 cup	warm soy milk

Beat by hand the molasses, oil and milk. Then add dry ingredients.

Batter should be light and spill into an 8" x 8" pan like one big cookie.

Sprinkle a handful of sesame seeds on top.

Bake 350° for 40 minutes. Cool before serving.

Serve with a good quality margarine or lecithin spread.

Figgy Duff

Figgy Duff is a Traditional Newfoundland raisin pudding which is boiled in a cloth bag and served steaming hot. *Figgy* refers to the raisins; *duff* to the dough mixture (dough was some times pronounced *duff* in British dialect.)

2 cups	sifted flour
1 cup	raisins
1/2 cup	molasses
1/4 cup	oil or melted margarine
1 tsp.	baking soda
2 tbsp.	hot water
1 tsp.	egg replacer
1/2 cup	whole wheat flour
1 tsp.	ginger, allspice, and cinnamon
1/2 tsp.	sea salt

Combine dry ingredients first. Mix water with egg replacer and add to dry ingredients along with molasses and oil. Fold raisins into mixture. Spoon the dough into a pudding bag or mold. Place mold in steamer or large pot. Add boiling water halfway up sides of pudding mold.

Cover and steam for two hours or until firm to touch.

If you are using a cloth pudding bag place bag in enough boiling water to cover bag.

When cooked, immediately open bag and place pudding on a serving dish.

Molasses Coady to pour over pudding before serving:

1 cup	molasses
1/4 cup	water
1/4 cup	margarine
1 tbsp.	lemon juice

In a saucepan combine above ingredients. Bring to a boil then simmer for 10 minutes. Serve hot over pudding.

A KEY TO MAKING LIGHT BREAD IS TO KNEAD IT WELL. ALWAYS USE FRESH YEAST. KEEP THE DOUGH WARM AND LET IT RISE IN AN AREA THAT HAS NO DROUGHTS.

Pita Bread

In a small bowl pour 1 cup warm water.

Stir in 1 tsp. honey.

Sprinkle 1 1/2 tsp. yeast over the water.

Allow to dissolve and rise for ten minutes.

In a large bowl measure:

1 tsp.	sea salt
3 cups	flour

When yeast has risen, add an additional tablespoon of honey before adding to flour.

Mix flour and yeast thoroughly with a wooden spoon. Knead 10 minutes adding more flour as you knead to prevent dough from sticking to bowl.

Oil bowl, cover and let rise 1 1/2 hours in a warm place.

Punch dough and knead again 5 minutes. On a floured board divide into 6 equal parts.

Preheat oven to 475°

Form into smooth round balls. Cover with clean towel and let stand for 15 minutes. Roll to 1/4" thickness. Place on ungreased baking tray.

Bake on lowest possible oven rack for 10 minutes or until puffed and brown. Serve fresh.

Wrap the freshly baked breads in a towel and place in a brown paper bag for 15 minutes. This serves to maintain their thin pockets as they deflate, preventing them from crumbling into crackers.

Tofu Herb Rolls*

16 oz.	soft tofu
1 tbsp.	yeast
1/2 cup	warm water
1 tsp.	sea salt
1/2 tsp.	dill weed
1/2 tsp.	chives
1 tsp.	minced onion
1/2 tsp.	minced garlic
3–3 1/2	cups flour
2 tbsp.	margarine
1 tbsp.	honey
1/2 cup	sesame seeds

Drain tofu. Sprinkle yeast in a bowl with water and honey. Add sea salt, dill, chives, onion, and garlic, plus 1 cup flour. Mix well. Mash tofu into mixture. Add margarine. Gradually add remaining flour until you obtain a dough of medium consistency. Knead until smooth and elastic (about 10 minutes). Place in an oiled bowl and cover with a cloth. Let rise until double in bulk. Punch down and let rest 15 minutes. Form into balls (or desired shape) and roll in sesame seeds. Place on oiled baking sheet and let rise again until double in bulk. Bake at 375° for 20 minutes. Cool on a wire rack.

*Recipe by Sheila Moore, dedicated to the Waterford Bridge Road Vegans, from the 1988 edition of Mary Jane's newsletter, *The Scoop*.

Corn Meal Bun or Bread

Stir together:

1 cup	corn meal
1 cup	soy and rice flour combination
2 tsp.	baking powder
1 tsp.	protein seasoning or sea salt
1 tsp.	honey dissolved in 1/2 cup warm water

Add:

1 cup	nut milk (soy or almond)
1/4 cup	light oil

Spoon into muffin tins or a loaf pan.

Bake 375° for 15-20 minutes.

Figgie Lizzie Tea Buns*

Preheat oven to 400°

In a medium size bowl measure:

2 cups	water or soy milk
1/3 cup	sunflower oil
1/3 cup	raw sugar
1 tbsp.	lecithin (liquid or granular)
1 tsp.	Protein Seasoning

In a mixing bowl empty:

6 cups	light flour
1 1/2 cups	raisins
2 tbsp.	baking powder

Add liquid mixture to dry and stir batter until all is well combined.

Put on a floured table or board, roll lightly to 1" thickness and cut in 2" diameter circles with small glass or circular cookie cutter.

Place on cookie sheet almost joining buns to each other. Bake for 20 minutes.

Break open to test for a perfectly baked bun. Buns may be turned on to a cloth and separated from each other. Delicious with lecithin spread, or margarine (for old times sake). Serve with tea or my favourite hot drink, coffee substitute. Treat yourself now.

*This recipe originally came from my mother who learnt it from her mother, Mabel Hall, who came here from Failsworth, England. Through a roommate in Ottawa, Kathleen Small, it ended up on the menu of an international ambassadors conference in Peking, China, and was so enjoyed that several ambassadors asked to have the recipe for their kitchen tea menu.

Lightweight Bran Muffins

Preheat oven to 375°.

In a bowl combine:

3 cups	bran
2 cups	whole wheat flour
1 tbsp.	no-alum (low-sodium) baking powder
1 tsp.	allspice
1 tsp.	cloves
1/2 cup	chopped walnuts
1 cup	pitted dates chopped fine

In another bowl combine:

1 cup	nutmilk (a little more if too dry)
2 tbsp.	sunflower oil
1 tsp.	pure vanilla
1/2 cup	honey or molasses

Combine wet mixture with dry ingredients.

Spoon into oiled muffin tins.

Bake for 30 minutes.

Honey Scones

Sift together:

1 cup	whole-wheat flour
1/4 cup	soy flour
3/4 cup	rolled oats, blended or fine oat flour
1 tsp.	baking powder
1/4 tsp.	sea salt

Mix 2 tbsp. oil into the flour with your fingers until lumpy:

In a separate bowl whiz together.

1/2 cup	water
1/4 cup	soy milk powder
2 tbsp.	honey or maple syrup

Mix with dry ingredients until damp. Add just enough flour to enable you to roll dough out.

Divide into 2 parts, 1/2" thick. Trim off the rough edges and cut into four wedges. Prick the dough and heat up your frying pan. Oil the pan with a few drops of oil and lightly flour the dough.

Bake the scones slowly over a light to moderate heat with a lid on for about 5 minutes Turn them and bake on the other side for 5 minutes. Watch them, they can burn easily.

Serve warm with homemade jam.

*Margaret Atwood Wheat Germ Muffins Revised and Edited

Preheat oven to 375°.

Whiz in food processor:

1/3 cup	oil (corn or sunflower)
3/4 cup	honey
2 tsp.	lecithin (liquid or granular)
2 cups	soy milk
2 cups	combination of rice and whole wheat flour
2 tsp.	baking soda
2 tsp.	baking powder
1 tsp.	protein seasoning
1 1/2 tsp.	pure vanilla
2 cups	wheat germ

Combine liquid ingredients first, then add dry.

Do not over blend.

Fold in 1 cup partridge berry or blueberry, (fresh or frozen).

Bake for 20 minutes.

Yield: 20.

I originally found *Margaret Atwood Wheat Germ Muffins* in the Light Hearted *Canadian Literature Foodbook* and revised and edited the ingredients to suit my dietary regime.

Quidi Vidi Road Soup Biscuits

Preheat oven to 350°.

1 1/2 cups	durum flour
1 tsp.	broth and seasoning
1 tbsp.	no alum baking powder

cut in

4 tbsp.	sunflower oil
1/2 cup	honey

Add enough water or soy milk to make stiff consistency.

Spoon onto cookie sheet and flatten with a wet fork.

Bake for 20 minutes.

Makes 14 fluffy biscuits to serve with stew or soup.

WHEN MAKING MUFFINS, IF THERE IS NOT ENOUGH BATTER TO FILL ALL THE MUFFIN HOLES, FILL THE EMPTY ONES WITH WATER. THIS KEEPS THE TEMPERATURE EVEN WHILE BAKING.

Doyle's Zucchini Loaf

Preheat oven to 350°.

2 cups	flour
1 tsp.	baking powder
1 tsp.	baking soda
1/2 tsp.	sea salt
2 tsp.	cinnamon
1/2 tsp.	nutmeg
2 tsp.	egg replacer dissolved in 2 tbsp. water
1/2 cup	corn or sunflower oil
1 cup	raw sugar
1 cup	grated zucchini
1 tsp.	pure vanilla
1/2 cup	chopped walnuts (optional)

Beat together: Oil, sugar, egg replacer, vanilla and zucchini.

In another bowl sift remaining dry ingredients.

Combine with zucchini mixture and stir well.

Pour into oiled loaf pan or bread pan and bake for 50 minutes. When cooked the top of the loaf will crack slightly. Let stand in loaf pan 10 minutes before removing from pan. Cool on rack before slicing.

Special Occasion Pancakes

In a bowl measure:

1 cup	unbleached white flour
1/2 cup	rice flour
1/2 cup	soy flour
3 tsp.	no aluminum baking powder
pinch	protein seasoning

Hand blend:

1 tbsp.	corn oil
1 tbsp.	honey
1 tsp.	liquid lecithin

Make a canyon hole in centre of flour mixture and add blended ingredients.

Add milk, approximately 2 cups, until mixture becomes easy to stir. Lumpy batter works best.

Fry evenly, serve with maple syrup or la confiture.

Magic Potion Apple Pancakes (1986)

(Anahareo and my nephew, Django, made magic potions while I made these)

Mix these flours:

1 cup	millet flour
1 cup	organic corn flour
1/2 cup	soy flour
1/2 cup	lima bean or brown rice flour
1 tsp.	cinnamon
1/2 tsp.	nutmeg
4 tsp.	no-alum baking powder

Blend:

4 cups	soy milk (use fresh soy milk or make milk by blending 3 tbsp. soy bean milk powder with 4 cups water)
1 tbsp.	corn oil
1 tbsp.	honey

Combine all of the above.

Add 1/2 cup raisins and 1 grated apple.

Makes a thin batter, not unlike a crepe.

Fry on medium heat until bubbles show through.

Turn and fry other side.

Serve with raspberry sauce, tahini spread and maple syrup.

Scorpio Sun Celebration Pancakes

1 cup	corn meal
1 cup	brown rice flour
1 cup	wheat germ
1 cup	sifted whole wheat or millet flour
1/2 cup	oat flakes
1/2 tsp.	cinnamon
4 tsp.	no-alum baking powder
4 cups	soy milk
1 tbsp.	liquid lecithin
2 tbsp.	light oil
2 tbsp.	honey
1/4 tsp.	protein seasoning

Combine and fry evenly. Serve with almond butter spread and maple syrup.

Yesteryear Pancakes For Today's Diet

Whiz together:

1 tbsp.	light oil
1 tbsp.	unrefined honey
1 tsp.	cinnamon
2 cups	warm soy or almond milk

Measure

2 cups	durum flour
1 tbsp.	no-alum baking powder

Combine the blended ingredients with the flour.

Aim for the consistency of a light pancake batter.

Fry evenly for the treat of your dairyless pancake days.

Serve with Quebec maple syrup.

Before frying you can vary the recipe by adding 1 cup blueberries, raisins or other small, seedless berry.

Heavenly Crepes

1 cup	unbleached white flour
2 tbsp.	egg replacer mixed with
1/4 cup	water
1 cup	soy milk
1 tbsp.	sunflower oil
1 tbsp.	honey

Combine all ingredients in a blender or Food Processor.

Heat a skillet over a medium heat.

Pour in 1 tsp. oil per crepe.

Add 1/2 cup batter to pan, tilting so the batter will cover the surface.

Cook until bottom of crepe is golden brown. Turn and briefly cook other side.

Remove crepe from pan and spread with almond or sesame butter. Fill crepes with apple sauce. Fold away from you & pour a dallop of *Soy Cream*(pg. 80), and a dribble of maple syrup on top of crepe.

Savory Crepes

Make crepe the same as above.

To make *Tofu Scrambler Filling*, sauté the following:

1	onion (diced)
1/2 lb.	tofu (mashed)
1/2 cup	mushrooms, cut small
1	garlic clove (crushed)
1/2 tsp.	savory & thyme combination

1 tsp.	protein seasoning
1 tbsp.	nutritional yeast flakes
1 tsp.	mineral bouillon or soy sauce

Fill crepes with Tofu Scrambler & roll away from you.

Serve with Garden Salad.

Pie Crust That Works

(with thanks to wax paper).

Makes 1 double pie crust.

2 1/2 cups	flour (1 rice, 1 1/2 unbleached white)
1/3 cup	spring water
2/3 cup	light oil
1 1/4 tsp.	salt substitute

Sift flours together.

Mix oil and water together.

Add all at once to flour.

Use a fork to stir lightly and form into a ball.

Roll between wax paper and flip in to pie plate.

Ready for apples, blueberries, or other fruit filling.

Amelia's Raspberry Turnovers

Prepare *Pie Crust That Works*, or use leftover pastry from a pie.

For every cup of raspberries use 1/2 cup honey.

Combine raspberries and honey.

Roll out pastry and cut in 2 1/2" squares.

Add 1 or 2 tbsp of raspberries in the middle of the square. Fold corner to corner.

Press edges with a fork, and prick surface of dough to allow steam to escape.

Bake at 400° for 20-30 minutes.

No Tricks Pumpkin Pie

Steam until soft:

| 3 cups | pumpkin (per pie) put through a sieve |

Add and mix:

1/2 cup	raw sugar or maple syrup
1 tsp.	cinnamon
1/2 tsp.	ginger
1/4 tsp.	nutmeg and cloves
1 cup	soy milk
1 tbsp.	egg replacer or corn flour

Pour into unbaked pie shell.

Bake at 400° for 30 minutes.

Raspberry Tofu "Cheesecake" or Pie

For best results, do not use a soft tofu. Medium works best.

Preheat oven to 375°.

Prepare and bake two 9" round graham cracker pie shells for crust. To make your life easier, when possible use a cheese cake pan.

Blend in a food processor or blender:

3 lbs.	tofu
1 1/2 cups	brown sugar or maple syrup
1/4 cup	fresh lemon juice
1/4 cup	light oil
1 tbsp.	vanilla
	pinch of sea salt

Pour into baked pie shells and bake for 1 hour. Crust will slightly crack when done.

Chill and prepare a raspberry sauce for the topping.

From Another Time Apple Pie

Have ready a *Pie Crust That Works*

You will need:

2 lbs.	apples per pie (thinly sliced)
1/2 cup	honey
31/2 tbsp.	arrowroot powder
2 tsp.	lemon juice
2 tsp.	coriander
1/4 tsp.	sea salt

Cook apples lightly for a few minutes in a 1/4 cup water.

Drain liquid and retain.

Add arrowroot to liquid. Stir until smooth.

Add this to apples. Then add coriander, lemon and honey.

Put filling in pie crust.

Cover with top crust.

Seal with a fork and cut your favourite design on top.

Bake for 30 minutes at 400° until golden brown.

Wild Blueberry Pie

Make pastry for 2 pie crusts.

Preheat oven to 400°.

Filling:

4 cups	wild fresh blueberries
1/2 cup	honey
1/2 tsp.	nutmeg
1/2 tsp.	cinnamon
3 tbsp.	cornstarch or arrowroot flour
1 tbsp.	lemon juice
2 tbsp.	margarine

Roll out half the pastry. Line pie plate and trim pastry larger than rim. Toss blueberries with nutmeg, cinnamon, cornstarch and lemon juice. Pour into pie shell, mound up slightly in the middle. Spread honey over berries. Dot with margarine. Roll out rest of pastry and cover berry filling. Fold edge of bottom crust over edge of top crust, press together. Design the top crust (with holes — made with a fork — to allow steam to escape). Bake for 30 minutes, or until crust is golden brown ar '
filling begins to bubble.

M.F. White

Blueberries and Chanderelles

The Eldamar Cookbook

Main Dishes with Trimmings

Naeme's Tofu Burgers _____ 38

Vegie Burgers _____ 38

The Tacky Taco _____ 39

Spinach or Cabbage Enchiladas _____ 39

Tempeh Casserole _____ 40

Choux-fleur au Gratin _____ 41

Benyard Scalloped Potatoes _____ 42

Quick Summer's Meal For Three _____ 42

Baked Brown Rice _____ 42

Vegie Paté à Lorraine _____ 43

Tofu Style Lasagna _____ 44

Eggplant Comes Around _____ 45

Moussaka _____ 45

Shepardless Pie _____ 46

Nutritional Yeast Sauce _____ 46

Soy Loaf _____ 47

Spanokapita de Sandrosco _____ 47

Sandrosco's Chick-Pea Festive Loaf _____ 48

Wild Chanterelle Stew _____ 48

Millet Pie _____ 49

Festive Barbecue Gluten _____ 50

Cabbage Rolls _____ 51

More Than A Pot Pie _____ 52

Chili Sans Carne _____ 53

Everybody's Ginger Stir Fry _____ 53

Belly Full Baked Beans _____ 54

Stuffed Zucchini _____ 54

Dandelion Scoff _____ 55

Tofu and Spinach Quiche _____ 55

Scallop (Gluten) Casserole _____ 56

Fettucini in a Marian White Sauce _____ 56

Karmafree Vegetable Curry _____ 58

TRIMMINGS

Pagan Vegan Gravy _____ 59

No Fuss Chips _____ 59

Stuffing For Its Own Sake _____ 59

Lyly's Sweet Relish _____ 60

Come From Away Piccalilli Relish _____ 60

Rice Dumplings _____ 61

Soka _____ 61

Tofu Coating For Baking Or Frying _____ 61

Connie's Potato Dip _____ 62

Devilled Eggless Sandwich _____ 62

Steve's Salsa _____ 62

Naeme's Tofu Burgers

2 lbs.	firm, organic tofu
1 small	onion, minced fine
4 tbsp.	fresh carrot, schedded fine
1 tbsp.	minced red pepper (optional)
	pinch thyme and basil crumbled fine.
2 tbsp.	nutritional yeast + 1 tbsp. Protein Seasoning
2 tbsp.	chick pea flour or potato flour

Have ready:
Pita breads, lettuce or alfalfa sprouts, dill pickle and oil for frying.

» Freeze tofu. This is the secret of this recipe.

» Thaw tofu (takes a day) and squeeze out excess water, through a cloth.

» Mix all ingredients (except pita bread, lettuce, sprouts & pickles, of course.) This is fairly crumbly. A burger patty maker would eliminate a lot of grief in this next step, or use your hands and form into burgers. Makes 12-14 depending on your ideal burger size.

» Fry at a meduim heat until golden on each side.

» Heat Pita breads in moderate oven only long enough to soften them. Cut off top. Stuff with the tofu burger and your favorite burger dressings.

My personal fave —
» Spread mustard on one side of pita and soyanaise on other. Put in burger, sliced tomato, sliced dill pickle, slice of soy cheese, ketchup and stuff with alfalfa sprouts or lettuce leaves.

» Serve with natural flavour sodas.

Veggie Burgers

Soak 2 cups rolled oats in just enough soy milk to cover. Let stand for 20 minutes.
Add

1 cup	cooked rice
1/2 cup	finely chopped onion
1/2 cup	grated carrot
1 cup	ground sunflower seed
1 tsp.	parsley and thyme
2 cloves	garlic
1 tbsp.	Protein Seasoning
1 tbsp.	nutritional yeast
2 tbsp.	soy sauce
2 tbsp.	egg replacer

Mix together and form into 2" patties and dip in cornmeal.

Fry on both sides in a good quality oil.

Serve with **Lyly's Relish** and **No Fuss Chips** on the side.

The Tacky Taco

Chop:

1 med.	onion
1 med.	tomato
6 leaves	lettuce

Set aside in individual bowls.

Fry on medium heat:

2 cups	cooked and mashed (pinto or kidney) beans in
2 tbsp.	olive oil

Season with:

1 tsp.	chili pepper
1 tbsp	Protein Seasoning

Spoon into taco shells

Grate soy cheese to put over beans or *Nutritional Yeast Sauce.*

Bake at 350° for 10 minutes.

Serve with *Steve's Salsa* and chopped vegies sprinkled over the top.

Spinach or Cabbage Enchiladas

1 1/2 lb.	spinach or cabbage
3 tbsp.	olive oil
1 cup	onion, diced fine
2 cloves	garlic, minced or pressed
1 tbsp.	Protein Seasoning
1/2 lb.	grated carrot, mixed with
1/2 cup	nutritional yeast and 1 tbsp. lemon
1 tsp.	Bernard Jensen Broth or Seasoning
10	fresh corn tortillas

Method:

Wash, drain and chop spinach or cabbage. Heat oil in a large cast iron pot, sauté onion & garlic till golden. Add cabbage (or spinach) and toss in hot oil until tender. Add Protein Seasoning and continue cooking over medium heat, stirring often, until all liquid is gone.

Brush a tortilla with olive oil.

Heat tortilla quickly in a frying pan.

Spread a heaping tbsp. of soy cheese or *Nutritional Yeast Sauce* in the centre.

Spread a tbsp. of spinach mixture over this. Fold and roll.

Oil a large casserole pot & arrange enchiladas in it.

Pour the followung heated sauce over these:

Sauce to heat:

1 tsp.	olive oil
1 tbsp.	Protein Seasoning
1 tbsp.	pea flour
1 cup	soy milk
1 cup	coconut cream melted in 2 tbsp. water
1/2 cup	diced chilies.

Pour sauce over rolled enchiladas.

Cover and bake at 350° for 10 minutes. Uncover for browning.

Tempeh* Casserole

Pour 1 tbsp. olive oil into a cast iron pot (preferably).

Dice & sauté

2 cups	onion
2 cloves	garlic
1 lb.	tempeh
2 med.	carrots
1 stalk	celery
1	small green pepper

Allow to simmer at medium heat for 15 minutes stirring occasionally.

Add a 1/4 cup water to prevent ingredients from sticking to the pot.

Meanwhile:

Blend 4 ripe tomatoes with 1 tbsp. molasses, add to sautéed ingredients.

When tender add 8 oz. spinach

Add the following herbs:

1 tsp.	basil
2 tsp.	thyme
1 tbsp.	B J's
1 tbsp.	Protein Seasoning
1 tsp.	unsalted mustard
1 tbsp.	lemon juice.

Sprinkle with nutritional yeast flakes before serving.

Suggestion:

Serve with butternut squash that has been baked, mashed and seasoned lightly with olive oil, herbs and cayenne pepper.

*Tempeh is fermented soy bean easily digested and nutritious.

Choux-fleur au gratin (Quebec style)

Have ready:

1 med.	cauliflower
2 med.	onions (chopped)
1 clove	garlic (pressed)
3 tbsp.	yellow pea flour
3 tbsp.	olive oil
2 cups	water
1 cup	soy cheese grated or *Nutritional Yeast Sauce*
1 cup	soy milk
1 tsp.	basil, parsley
1 tbsp.	Protein Seasoning
1 lb.	tofu (diced)
2 tbsp.	Soy sauce
1 cup	Croutons

Steam the cauliflower *for 5 minutes* (retain water)

Soak diced tofu in enough soy sauce to cover

Sauce:

Heat olive oil in a big frying pan and add diced onions and garlic. Fry on medium heat until onions are golden (not brown).

Add flour until all the oil is absorbed.

While stirring, add the water (left over from the cauliflower). Add soy milk a little at a time to prevent the formation of lumps in the sauce.

Cook until thick.

In another frying pan, sauté the diced tofu.

Layer the cauliflower pieces and the sautéed tofu in a casserole dish, top with the sauce. Sprinkle croutons on top and spread soy cheese or *Nutritional Yeast Sauce* over the top of the casserole.

Broil for 10 minutes (or until golden brown). Then, lower the temperature to 350° and bake for 20 minutes.

Bon appétit!!

Benyard Scalloped Potatoes

Preheat oven to 375°.

Wash and scrub 6 large potatoes, dry and thinly slice.

Place one layer of potatoes in oiled 9" x 12" baking pan.

Slice 1 large onion for second layer.

Sprinkle on each layer:

1 tsp.	parsley + 1 tsp. savory
1 tsp.	Protein Seasoning
1/2 tsp.	black pepper

Chop fine 1 small green pepper for middle layer.

Combine:

1/2	cup nutritional yeast
1 tbsp.	pea flour
1 tsp.	paprika and sprinkle over each layer.

Soak 6 oz. dulse or other seaweed (optional).

Drain and spread over onions.

Add 2 more layers of sliced potato and onions, seasoning, dulse and herbs. End with potatoes.

Pour 2 cups thick soy milk over casserole.

Bake for 35-45 minutes until tender.

Serve hot!

Suggestion:

For a complete meal serve with a spinach salad or steamed green beans marinated in apple cider vinegar, olive oil and Protein Seasoning.

Quick Summer's Meal for Three

Bake a medium whole butternut squash (or other variety) at 400° for 40 minutes
Meanwhile marinate slices of tofu. See *Tofu Coating For Baking*.

Before serving squeeze juice of a lemon over tofu and a sprinkling of thyme.

Serve with steamed swiss chard, seasoned steamed rice or *Baked Brown Rice*.

Baked Brown Rice

2 tbsp.	oil
1 cup	finely chopped onion
1 cup	finely chopped celery
1 cup	brown rice
21/2 cups	vegetable stock
1/2 cup	grated carrot
1/2 cup	sliced mushrooms

1/8 tsp.	thyme
1/8 tsp.	dried marjoram
3/4 tsp.	Protein Seasoning
1/8 tsp.	black pepper

Heat oven to 350°

Heat oil in large saucepan.

Add onion and celery and stir over medium heat until limp.

Remove from heat, stir in remaining ingredients and pour into oiled casserole.

Cover and bake for 50 minutes. Uncover, stir with a fork and bake until rice is tender and moisture has all been absorbed. (about 10 more minutes.)

Vegie Paté à Lorraine*

Preheat oven to 350°.

Method:

Using a food processor blend until fine:

| 2 1/2 cups | flour (rice, pea, and soy) with |
| 1 1/2 cups | sunflower seeds or 1 cup sunflower & 1/2 cup sesame seeds |

In a large stainless steel bowl measure:

2 cups	nutritional yeast
1 tsp.	thyme, basil and oregano (each)
1 tbsp.	Protein Seasoning
1 tsp.	Newfoundland savory

Combine dry ingredients.

In a food processor blend until smooth:

1/4 cup	lemon juice
1 cup	sunflower oil or other light oil
6 med.	onions
3 large	potatoes
1/4 cup	tamari soy sauce

Combine wet ingredients with dry mixture.

Add up to 2 1/2 cups boiled water (allowed to cool a little before pouring over mixture).

Mix well and pour into one lightly oiled 9" x 12" pan & one 5" x 8" pan.

Makes two 1" loaves.

Bake for 50 minutes. Cool before cutting.

*Lorraine Desjardins shared this recipe with me when I had the good fortune of sharing my home with her for almost a year. She revised the original recipe from her father's French Paté which I have in turn revised once again. Please do not freeze the paté as this alters the delicate paté flavour.

Tofu Style Lasagna

You will need to boil a large pot of water for the lasagna noodles. When the water has come to a rolling boil, cook 1 pkg. (approximately 1 lb.) lasagna noodles (reduce heat to medium high and cook for 12-15 minutes until tender. Drain and cover with cold water to prevent noodles from sticking together.

While the noodles are cooking make the following tomato sauce. Sauté:

1/4 cup	olive oil
1 large	diced onion
1 large	diced green pepper
2 stalks	celery, diced
1 clove	garlic, diced
1 cup	sliced mushrooms
2 cups	tomato sauce
6 cups	blended tomatoes

Add:

1/2 tsp.	oregano, basil and parsley
1 tbsp.	Protein Seasoning

Simmer over low heat for 20 minutes.

Have ready 1 lb. fresh spinach, chopped fine.

Tofu Filling Mash:

2 lb.	firm tofu and season with
1 tbsp.	Protein Seasoning
1 tbsp.	tamari soy sauce
2 tbsp.	lemon juice

Preheat oven to 350°.

Method:

In a 9" x 13" pan place a small amount of tomato sauce and spread evenly over the pan.

Add a layer of the cooked noodles, and a layer of spinach.

Spread a little of the tofu filling over the noodles and begin again with the tomato sauce, noodles, tofu and spinach.

End with sauce.

Spread 1 cup *Nutritional Yeast Sauce* over lasagna or grated soy cheese.

Bake for 30 minutes.

Suggestion: Serve with *Chlorophyll Garden Salad.*

Eggplant Comes Around

Slice 2 small or 1 large eggplant into 1/2" pieces.

Brush with oil and sprinkle on 1 tbsp. Protein Seasoning.

Broil until lightly brown.

Turn and brown other side.

Soak:

1 cup	TVP (texturized vegetable protein) in
1 cup	water (see *Soy Loaf* page 47 to make your own TVP)

Meanwhile make a tomato sauce:

In a sauce pan *Simmer:*

2 cups	blended tomatoes
1 tbsp.	tahini
1 tbsp.	nutritional yeast
1 tbsp.	mineral bouillon
1 tbsp.	basil, thyme, and chili (combined)
1 tbsp.	Protein Seasoning
1 tsp.	Bernard Jensen Broth or Seasoning

Oil a large baking dish.

Layer bottom with eggplant.

Sprinkle TVP over the eggplant and then add 1 cup tomato sauce over first layer.

Add second layer of eggplant & TVP, ending with sauce.

Bake at 350° for 40 minutes. Serve hot.

Moussaka

2 large eggplant sliced 1/2" thick.

Sprinkle with Protein Seasoning.

Put paper towels between each layer and place a heavy cutting board on top to press out the water.

Tomato Sauce:

Sauté in olive oil 3 med onions, 2 cloves garlic.

Add:

1/2 tsp.	mint
1 tbsp.	parsley
1 tbsp.	honey
1/4 tsp.	pepper
2 cups	tomato paste
2 cups	warm water

Simmer for 15 minutes.

Topping:

1 lb.	soy cream cheese or 2 cups *Nutritional Yeast Sauce*

| 1/2 tsp. | rosemary, mace, pepper, |
| 2/3 tsp. | cloves |

Brush eggplant with oil and brown in frying pan. Place in baking casserole dish and spoonsauce over eggplant.

Add topping.

Bake for 40 minutes at 350°.

Shepherdless Pie

Preheat oven to 350°.

Scrub and steam 10 med. Newfoundland Blue potatoes.

Meantime:

Sauté in 2 tbsp. hot olive oil:

1	large onion
1/2	green pepper
2 stalks	celery
2 cloves	home grown garlic

Add:

1/4 tsp.	thyme, savory, basil, and oregano (each)
1 lb.	mashed tofu
1 tbsp.	tamari

Set aside when nicely brown.

Next have on hand:

| 16 oz. | steamed corn cut from cob |

Method:

Mash steamed potatoes adding a little soy milk, Protein Seasoning, olive oil and black pepper.

In a large casserole dish spread the sautéed tofu evenly along pan.

Next, spread the corn and top with all the mashed potatoes.

Bake for 20 minutes.

Serve with fresh steamed broccoli, local carrots, and *Pagan Vegan Gravy.*

Nutritional Yeast Sauce

Combine:

1 cup	nutritional yeast flakes
1/2 cup	apple cidar vinegar
1 tbsp.	wet mustard
1 tsp.	Protein Seasoning

Add just enough water to make a creamy consistency — one that will pour over your casserole dish.

Soy Loaf

4 cups	soy pulp*
2 cups	whole wheat or rice and soy flour
1 cup	wheat germ
3/4 cup	nutritional yeast flakes
2 1/2 tsp.	fennel seed or ground fennel
1 tbsp.	black pepper
3 tsp.	oregano
2 tsp.	Protein Seasoning
2 tbsp.	garlic minced
2 tbsp.	prepared mustard
2 tsp.	allspice
1 1/4 cup	soy milk
1/4 cup	tamari or mineral bouillon

Mix ingredients well.

Oil loaf pans.

Fill and cover. Steam for 1 1/2 hr.

Let sit until cool. Slice and fry as a side dish or mash to use in spaghetti or chili recipes.

*Make soy pulp by soaking 1 lb. soy beans over night, drain and put through a grinder or champion juicer. Boil a kettle of hot water and put pulp in a large boiler. Simmer for 30 minutes. Stir to prevent from sticking. Allow to cool and squeeze the pulp through a cheese cloth to obtain soy milk. The remaining pulp you can use fresh, as in this recipe, or spread on a large cookie sheet and bake for 40 minutes. This product is called TVP, texturized vegetable protein.

Spanokapita de Sandrosco

Preheat oven to 375°.

Take 1 sheet filo pastry.

Brush with melted margarine.

Prepare 6 layers like this.

Sauté for 10 minutes:

1 cup	onions
1 lb.	mashed tofu
1 tbsp.	Protein Seasoning
1 lb.	chopped spinach

Put between each layer of filo.

Repeat until the casserole dish is full (6 layers).

Sprinkle 1 tbsp. *Nutritional Yeast Sauce* on top.

Bake at 375° for 40 minutes or until golden brown.

Sandrosco's Chick-Pea Festive Loaf

Soak overnight 4 cups chick peas. Cook until soft (takes 2-3 hours).

Grind chick peas in a food processor, blender or juicer (using blank instead of juicing grid).

Sauté:

2 cups	diced onion
1 stalk	diced celery
1/2	diced green pepper
2 cloves	diced garlic

Add to the sautéed mixture and fry:

1 cup	tahini
1 tsp.	thyme
1 tbsp.	Newfoundland savory
1 tbsp.	Protein Seasoning
1/4 cup	dried parsley
1	bay leaf (remove before baking)

Grate in a separate bowl:

1/2 loaf	bread to crumbs.

Add enough hot water to cover crumbs.

Season with

1/2 cup	tamari
2 tbsp.	Bernard Jensen's Broth and Seasoning

Combine the sautéed mixture with bread crumbs and ground chick peas.

Place in oiled loaf pans and bake at 325° for 1 1/2 hours.

Serve with *Pagan Vegan Gravy, Stuffing*, fresh vegetables, and cranberry sauce.

Wild Chanterelle Stew

In a cast iron frying pan place 1 lb. fresh wild chanterelle mushrooms. Simmer on medium heat until liquid escapes from mushrooms. Drain off liquid. Put mushrooms in a separate bowl.

Next sauté in olive oil or other vegetable oil:

1	large onion
1 stalk	celery
1/2	med. green pepper
2 cloves	garlic, minced
1/2 tsp.	oregano, thyme, savory (each)
1 lb.	gluten wheatlets (chopped)
Add	chanterelle mushrooms

Meanwhile chop:

2	large carrots
3	large potatoes

| 1 | med. parsnip |
| 4 leaves | swiss chard or other green vegie (chopped) |

Add to Sauté mixture and stir in 1 cup warm water.

Stew for 10 minutes.

In a measuring cup combine:

| 3 tbsp. | yellow pea flour |
| 1 cup | water (gradually) to form paste |

Stir this into bubbling stew until it is well mixed.

Reduce heat to medium low and add more liquid as needed to make gravy consistency.

Season with 2 tbsp. Protein Seasoning and 1 tsp. minerial bouillon.

Ready to eat when vegies are tender. Do not over cook. Serve with *Quidi Vidi Soup Biscuits or Rice Dumplings.*

Millet Pie

Preheat oven at 350°.

Cook 1 cup millet in 2 1/2 cups water for 20 minutes.

You will need:

1 cup	rolled oats
2 tbsp.	corn oil
1 cup	chopped onion
4 tbsp.	tamari
1 cup	mushrooms, cut
1 tsp.	basil and parsley
2 tbsp.	nutritional yeast
1 cup	vegetable broth

Sauté onions in large frying pan.

Add mushrooms and rolled oats and stir well.

Add millet, seasoning, and vegetable broth.

Season to taste with garlic, paprika, cayenne, and thyme.

While it is simmering, prepare a *Pie Crust That Works.*

Fill pie crust and put pastry top over *Millet Pie.*

Bake for 35 minutes. Serve with *Pagan Vegan Gravy.*

Festive Barbecue Gluten

This unusual and tasty dish is derived from the original Gluten Rib recipe found in the *Farm Vegetarian Cookbook*.

First you must make the pot of gluten:

6 cups	unbleached white flour
2 cups	whole wheat
2 cups	gluten flour
	(or you can omit the whole wheat and add 2 more cups of gluten flour which makes the gluten a lot more tender)
3 cups	cold water. Combine with flour to make a stiff dough.

Knead for 15 minutes until the dough feels expansive and flexible. Put in a large stainless steel bowl and cover with cold water.

Let soak for at least 2 hours.

Begin by kneading it under *cold* water, discarding the water as it turns milky. This removes the starch from the flour and what remains is the gluten. Keep the dough together. If it begins to fall apart you're in trouble! Change water as it fills with the white starch. Stop kneading when water is only slightly starchy looking.

Reserve this gluten (8 cups) for the following recipe:

Have ready:

6-8 cups	fresh gluten
1/3 cup	nutritional yeast flakes
2 tbsp.	peanut butter
1 tbsp.	paprika
1 tbsp.	Protein Seasoning
1 medium	onion, chopped and Sautéed in
1/2 cup	vegetable oil

Method:

Drain off any excess water from gluten and combine with your hands the yeast flakes, peanut butter and seasonings in the bowl with the gluten.

Pour hot onions and oil over the gluten.

Using your hands begin to mix the gluten. As the oil breaks the gluten down it will get a little stringy.

Tear off chunks of the gluten (3 X 6" pieces) and place in a large, well oiled baking pan.

Bake at 350° for 1 hour. Gluten should be crispy and brown on the bottom.

While baking prepare the following sauce:

In a large cast iron pot sauté the following:

1/4 cup	oil
1 large	diced onion

2 cloves	minced garlic
6 cups	tomato sauce
1/2 cup	water
1 tbsp.	molasses
1/2 cup	prepared mustard
1 tbsp.	Protein Seasoning
1 tsp.	allspice
2 tsp.	cayenne
2 tbsp.	parsley flakes

Bring sauce to a boil and then reduce heat, cover and simmer for 20 minutes. Stir occasionally.

Add 1 tbsp. tamari soy sauce and 1/4 cup fresh lemon juice.

Remove gluten from the oven and pour sauce over the entire pan. Don't spare the sauce.

Return to oven and bake for ten minutes longer.

Serve on a very special occasion.

For an extra festive meal serve with masked potatoes, any steamed green, garden carrots, turnip hash and *Pagan Vegan Gravy*.

Cabbage Rolls

yield 1 dozen

Preheat oven to 350°.

Roll Mixture:

1 medium	cabbage
1 cup	chopped onion
8 sliced	mushroom
1 cup	mashed tofu
1 cup	cooked rice
1 tbsp.	vegetable oil
1 bud	minced garlic
1 tbsp.	Protein Seasoning, pepper, thyme

Sauce:

1 tbsp.	oil
1 cup	tomato sauce
1 tbsp.	lemon juice
2 tbsp.	honey
1 tbsp.	tamari
2 tbsp.	corn flour
1 cup	vegie broth (liquid)

Mix in sauce pan. Stir in 2 tbsp. corn flour until thick.

Method:

Cut out cabbage heart and steam cabbage leaves for 10 minutes. Sauté onions, garlic, and mushrooms in oil. Add other ingredients and mix. Drop about 3 tbsp. of the mixture in the centre of the cabbage leaves and roll. Place rolls next to each other in oven proof casserole dish.

Pour sauce over the rolls and bake for 40 minutes.

More Than A Pot Pie

Dice and Sauté the following in 2 tbsp. olive oil.

1	onion
3	potatoes
2	parsnips
2	carrots
2	celery stalks
1 tsp.	thyme, savory and pepper mixture
1	bay leaf (remove before serving)

Combine the following in a bowl:

3 cups	flour
2 tsp.	Protein Seasoning
1 tsp.	savory
1 tsp.	baking soda
1 tsp.	baking powder
1 cup	soy milk
1 cup	water
1/3 cup	corn oil

Mix until well combined. This is the Pot Pie cover.

Meanwhile in a measuring cup combine:

1 tbsp.	Protein Seasoning
3 tbsp.	yellow pea flour

Gradually add warm water to make a thick paste.

Continue adding water, up to 2 cups.

Pour this smooth mixture into the pot. Stir well.

Add 1 cup peas, fresh or frozen.

Spoon dough over the top of the pot and bake at 350° for 30 minutes.

WILD HERBS TO COLLECT & USE IN RECIPES:
SPEARMINT, NETTLE (THE STING IS LOST IN
STEAMING), YARROW, PLANTAIN, WILD ROSE
PETALS, CLOVER, CHICKWEED.

Chili Sans Carne

Cook until soft 3 cups red kidney beans.

Beans cook faster if they have been soaked overnight in a stainless steel pot or glass bowl.

Meanwhile sauté in a cast iron pot:

2 tbsp.	oil
1 large	diced onion
1 large	diced green pepper
2 cloves	minced garlic
1 lb.	crumbled firm tofu
1 tbsp.	chili powder
1 tsp.	cumin
1 tbsp.	Protein Seasoning
1 cup	tomato sauce or 3 crushed tomatoes

Add the cooked beans to the pot with enough liquid to cover beans.

Simmer for 30 minutes. Serve hot with *Corn Meal Buns* and *Baked Brown Rice*.

Everybody's Ginger Stir Fry

Have on hand:

1 lb.	fresh broccoli
1/2 cup	fresh spinach
1/2 cup	fresh or frozen pea pods
4 stalks	celery
2 medium	onions
3 stalks	green onions
3/4 cup	water
1 tbsp.	mineral bouillon
1 tbsp.	corn starch
2 tbsp.	vegetable oil
1 tbsp.	minced fresh ginger root
1 tsp.	Protein Seasoning

Clean vegetables.

Cut broccoli tops and stalks into thin 2-inch strips. Chop spinach.

Remove ends and strings from pea pods.

Cut celery into 1/2 inch diagonal slices.

Cut onions into wedges.

Cut green onions into diagonal slices.

Combine water and bouillon.

Heat oil in wok over medium heat.

Add broccoli, onion wedges, ginger and Protein Seasoning.

Stir-fry 1 minute, add remaining vegetables and toss lightly.

Add water mixture. Toss until vegetables are completely coated.

Cook until liquid boils. Reduce heat. Cover wok and cook until vegetables are crisp-tender, 2 to 3 minutes. Serve over steamed rice.

Belly Full Baked Beans

Use 1 lb. navy beans for baking. Wash and take out any soiled beans. Soak over night in 1 qt. water.

Next morning use fresh waater to bring beans to a boil, and cook for 30 minutes.

Slice 2 med. onions and spread along bottom of bean crock.

Mix together:

1 tbsp.	Bernard Jensen's Broth or Seasoning
1/4 cup	apple cider vinegar
1 tsp.	mustard
1 tbsp.	honey
1/2 cup.	blackstrap molasses
1 cup	tomato paste
1/4 tsp.	black pepper
1 tsp.	Protein Seasoning

Once beans are boiled, drain (keeping liquid).

Layer onions in bottom of bean crock.

Pour sauce over onions and place beans over it.

Do not stir. Pour in just enough liquid to cover beans.

Cover and bake at 250° for 7 hours.

At end of 4 hours remove one cup of beans, mash and stir into other beans.

Put thin slices of tofu on top (optional).

Add liquid as needed to keep beans covered. 1 hr. before serving remove cover to brown tofu. Serve with *Corn Bread*.

Stuffed Zucchini

Preheat oven to 350°. You will need:

1	large zucchini
2 cups	cooked millet*
1 cup	onion sliced and sautéed
2/3 cup	fresh green peas partially cooked
1 cup	coarsely chopped spinach
1 tbsp.	roasted sesame seeds
1/4 cup	pine nuts
1 cup	chopped mushrooms
1 tbsp.	millet flour
1 tsp.	grated lemon rind

Wash zucchini and split down the middle, length wise, but not all the way through to the bottom skin. Open like a book and scoop out the seeds. Mix all ingredients together with cooked millet and stuff the zucchini. Close the zucchini and secure with string or a crisscross of tooth picks. Place in baking dish and bake until tender to fork (about 30 minutes). Remove from oven and place on a large platter. Surround with fresh sprigs of parsley and wedges of baked potatoes.

*How to cook millet

1 tbsp.	vegetable oil
1 cup	raw hulled millet
3 cups	boiling water
1/4 tsp.	sea salt

Pour millet into saucepan and add boiling water, sea salt and oil. Bring to a boil. Lower heat, cover and simmer until all the liquid is absorbed (about 25 minutes).

M.F. White

Beni Malone making Gluten

Scallop (Gluten) Casserole

Unless you make your own gluten, use 1 pkg. gluten scallops.

Sauté the following in 2 tbsp. olive oil:

2 med.	diced onions
1 med.	green pepper
1 stalk	celery
1 clove	garlic
1 tsp.	herb mixture (oregano, thyme, basil)

Add the cut scallops and continue to fry until tender and a little golden.

Meanwhile:

Chop 1 large carrot.

Finely cut 1/2 small cabbage and add to pot.

Stir often to prevent from sticking.

Simmer for 10-15 minutes.

Add:

3 tbsp.	Protein Seasoning
2 cups	water with 2 tbsp. corn starch. Stir well.

Casserole should look golden brown.

While it is cooking, boil water for spinach noodles.

Put a dollop of *Pesto* over noodles when they are cooked and strained.

Serve casserole over noodles with a tossed salad on the side.

Fettucini in a Marian White Sauce

Sauté:

1/2 cup	diced onion
1/2 cup	chopped celery in
2 tbsp.	olive oil
2 tbsp.	Protein Seasoning
1/2 tsp.	savory
1/4 tsp.	thyme

Add:

2 cloves	pressed garlic
1 lb.	diced tofu or tempeh

Fry for 5 minutes.

Add & Simmer:

1 cup	carrot short sticks
1/2 lb.	fresh chopped brocolli

Meanwhile boil a large pot of water for fettucini noodles.

In a measuring cup place 1/4 cup yellow pea flour. Stir in 2 cups soy milk. When smooth, add to Sautéed mixture & continue stirring until thick & creamy. If too thick add up to 1 cup spring water. (continued)

Remove sauce from heat and stir in

1/2 tbsp.	fresh parsley, chopped fine
1 tbsp.	mineral bouillon

Add 8 oz. cooked fettucine noodles to the sauce. Serve immediately with a dallop of *Pesto* over each serving.

Dandelion Scoff

Dandelion is a member of the sunflower family. Before the yellow flowers appear, the tender leaves are nature's first gift to us in the spring. The leaves contain an abundance of Vitamin A, iron & calcuim, and can be used as a blood purifier.

For a traditional meal with dandelion, prepare the following:

Collect —

1 lb.	fresh wild dandelion leaves

Wash well & separate from stem.

Meanwhile prepare a pot of vegetables: potatoes, carrots & turnips. Steam for 20 minutes. Add dandelion to the top of the steaming pot & continue to steam for another 20 minutes.

Serve with Pagan Vegan Gravy.

Tofu and Spinach Quiche

Preheat oven to 350°.

Have ready:

1	unbaked 8" pie shell

Sauté for 10 mins:

2 tbsp.	oil
2 medium	onion diced
2 lbs.	tofu, (crumble by hand, do not blend)
1/2 lb.	spinach
1	carrot grated fine
1/4 cup	nutritional yeast
3 tbsp.	fresh lemon juice
2 tbsp.	soy sauce
1 tbsp.	mustard
2 cloves	garlic
1/4 tsp.	black pepper
1 tbsp.	Protein Seasoning

Pour tofu mixture into pie shell. Bake for 45 minutes.

Allow to cool slightly before serving.

Karmafree Vegetable Curry

While you are preparing the curry spices and vegetables steam:

1 cup	organic long grain brown rice or basmati rice in
2 cups	boiled water and
1 tbsp.	sesame tahini

Cover and cook on a low heat for 50 minutes.

Meanwhile prepare the following chopped vegetables:

1 medium	onion
2 cloves	garlic
1 stalk	celery
1 small	green pepper
2 medium	carrot
1 medium	cauliflower
4 medium	potatoes
1 cup	peas

Sauté above first four ingredients in 2 tbsp. olive oil.

Measure and mix the following ground spices in a small bowl.

1 tbsp.	cumin
1 tbsp.	coriander
1 tbsp.	ginger
1 tbsp.	jamaican curry
1 tbsp.	madras curry
1 tbsp.	tumeric
2 tbsp.	protein seasoning
1 tsp.	cayenne pepper

Add spices all at once to the sautéed ingredients.

Simmer on a low heat for five minutes, add a small amount of water (no more than a cup) to moisten curry.

Next add chopped vegetables and continue to simmer until vegetables are tender. Stir often with a wooden spoon to prevent curry from sticking to the pot, add only enough water to keep curry moist. For a saltier curry, add 1 tbsp. tamari soy sauce before serving.

Serve over a bed of brown rice.

Trimmings to Accompany Main Dishes

Pagan Vegan Gravy

Almost every vegan I know has make their own version of this tasty gravy that can be served over a variety of vegetables and other dishes.

In a frying pan Sauté:

1	medium minced onion
1	garlic clove, diced

Stir in 1/4 tsp. of thyme and/or 1/4 tsp. savory.

The special ingredient is Protein Seasoning which gives the gravy its flavour. Use at least 3 heaping tbsp. for a large gravy.

Stir with a wooden spoon until the Protein Seasoning is absorbed by the oil.

In a measuring cup place 4 heaping tablespoons of yellow pea flour (or other flour). Begin to add water from your steamed vegetables, or if this is not available use up to 4 cups of spring water.

Stir mixture slowly into the pan and continue stirring to obtain a smooth gravy consistency.

When gravy is thick, add 1 tsp. of mineral bouillon or soy sauce.

Ready to serve over hot vegies. YUM!

No Fuss Chips

Preheat oven to 400°.

Slice potatoes as you would for french fries.

Remove middle rack from oven and layer with potato sticks.

Bake for 30 minutes (until browned & slightly crispy).

Remove from oven and put in a stainless steel bowl.

Season with a little olive oil, nutritional yeast flakes, apple cider vinegar and Protein Seasoning.

Stuffing For Its Own Sake

Blend or grate by hand 1/2 loaf of not-so-fresh whole wheat bread.

ADD:

1 1/2 tsp.	Newfoundland savory
1	onion chopped fine
1 1/2 tbsp.	margarine or olive oil
1 tsp.	Protein Seasoning

Mix together by hand.

Place in a small casserole dish & bake at 350° for 20 minutes.

Lyly's Sweet Relish

12	big cucumbers (do not peel)
12	big onions
1/4 cup	sea salt
1	green pepper
1	red pepper

Chop very small (use food processor or mill).

Let sit in its own juice for 2 hours.

Drain well.

Bring the following to a boil:

2 cups	vinegar
4 cups	raw sugar
1/2 tsp.	tumeric
1 tsp.	celery salt

Add cucumber mixture.

Boil for 1 hour.

Let cool.

Put in sterilized jars.

Come From Away Piccalilli Relish

Cooking time 45 minutes.

Chop and bring to a boil the following:

1 lb.	green tomatoes
1 lb.	red pepper
1 lb.	green pepper
1-2 tbsp.	hot pepper
1 lb.	onion
1 small	cabbage, cored, chopped
1 tsp.	Protein Seasoning
1 cup	honey
1 tbsp.	mustard seed and celery seed
1 cup	maple syrup (retain until relish is made)
2 cups	cider vinegar

Lower heat and cook 30 mins, stir occasionlly until thick.

Ladle vegies into hot canning mason jars, leaving 1/2" head space.

Pour syrup into each jar covering vegies and leaving 1/4" space, cover.

Process in boiling water for 10 minutes.

Remove from heat. Cool and check seals.

Label and store in cool dry place.

Rice Dumplings

1 1/3 cups	flour
1 cup	cooked rice
2 tsp.	Protein Seasoning + 1 tsp. B.J.'s
2 tbsp.	margarine
2/3 cup	soy milk
2 tsp.	baking powder
1 tbsp.	brown sugar

Mix all dry ingredients in a bowl. Cut in margarine until texture of meal. Stir in milk to make a sticky dough. Dust a large spoon with flour and spoon out 8-10 dumplings into gently simmering stew, spacing evenly. Cover pot tightly and simmer, without lifting lid for 15 minutes. Serve while hot.

Soka

This dish is a specialty from the south of France. It is normally made outdoors in hot ovens, but a very hot country oven will do; wood stoves work best.

Blend:

2 cups	chick pea flour with
3 cups	water

Pour on to baking sheet and pour a little olive oil over top.

Bake in super hot oven (at least 475°) until it resembles scrambled eggs.

Yum!

Tofu Coating For Baking or Frying

1 cups	flour
1 tsp.	pepper
1/2 tsp.	basil
1/2 tsp.	ginger
1 tbsp.	Protein Seasoning
2 tbsp.	paprika
1 tsp.	dry mustard
1/4 tsp.	thyme
1/4 tsp.	oregano
1 tbsp.	chili powder

Slice 1 lb. firm tofu 1/8" thick.

Dip each slice in soy milk and then role in the mixed dry ingredients. Deep fry each side for 2 minutes or broil until brown.

Connie's Potato Dip

2 cups	flour
1 tbsp.	pepper
1 tbsp.	Protein Seasoning
1 tsp.	basil
2 tbsp.	paprika
1 tbsp.	dry mustard
1/2 tsp.	thyme
1/2 tsp.	oregano
2 tbsp.	chili powder

Combine all ingredients.

Dip the potato wedges into water and then into the mixture.

Deep fry until golden brown.

For Tofu Pups or Tofu Hot Dogs dip into flour, then in soy milk, then into coating mixture. Deep fry and serve on a stick.

Devilled Eggless Sandwich

1/2 cup	tofu
1/4 cup	sliced green onion
1/4 cup	chopped celery
1 tsp.	Protein Seasoning

Mash tofu and add chopped celery, onion and Protein Seasoning.

Fold in tofunaise:

Blend 1/2 cup tofu with 1 tsp. oil, honey and BJ's. Add 1 minced clove of garlic. Mix well with mashed tofu.

Spread between two fresh slices of *Whole Wheat Protein Bread* and a leaf of lettuce.

Steve's Salsa

Blend lightly:

3 cups	tomatoes
2 tbsp.	olive oil
2 tbsp.	tamari
2 cloves	garlic
1 cup	onion
1/2 tsp.	chili powder
1 tbsp.	Protein Seasoning
1 tbsp.	cumin
1/2 tbsp.	coriander
1/2 tbsp.	cayenne
1/4 tsp.	black pepper

Serve with corn chips.

Desserts

Bitesize Friday Night Ginger Delights _____ 65

Hearty Oat And Raisin Cookies _____ 65

Oatmeal Drop Cookies_____ 66

Chocolate Cherry Volcanos _____ 67

Peanut Butter Gems _____ 67

First Grade Valentine Surprise_____ 68

Maxwell's Tofu Squares_____ 68

Greg's Lemon-Pineapple Squares _____ 69

Apricot Pudding _____ 69

Guilt Ridden Old Fashioned Chocolate Fudge From The Bay_____ 70

Doran's Fudge Pudding _____ 70

Welcome Home Blueberry Squares, 1984 _____ 71

Avondale Blueberry Dash _____ 71

Eldamar Blueberry Blunt _____ 72

Dock Ridge Partridge Berry Bog _____ 72

Apple Rhubarb Crisp _____ 73

Apple Pudding _____ 73

Elly Danica's Fresh Pear or Apple Tart _____ 74

Non-Traditional Strawberry Shortcake _____ 74

Christmas Pudding Bubbles Brown _____ 75

Irie Christmas Fruit Cake _____ 76

Carrot Cake _____ 77

Grandmother Hall's Apple Cake Extrodinaire_____ 77

Ginger-Pineapple Bake _____ 78

Anahareo's Raisin-nut Birthday Cake _____ 78

Watermelon Drink_____ 79

Vanilla Shakes A Winters Night _____ 79

Lavender Shake _____ 79

Carob Milkshake_____ 79

Nut Milk _____ 80

Soy Cream _____ 80

Banana Ice cream _____ 80

Vegatable Cocktail Party_____ 80

Bitesize Friday Night Ginger Delights

With a wooden spoon and mixing bowl stir these together:

1/4 cup	light oil
1 cup	honey
1 tsp.	liquid lecithin
1/4 cup	mild flavoured molasses

In a second bowl measure:

1/4 tsp.	sea salt
1/2 tsp.	cloves
1 tsp.	cinnamon
5 tsp.	ground ginger
2 cups	sifted flour
1 tsp.	baking soda

Combine all together and stir until smooth.

Mixture will be fairly dry.

Drop onto a floured board and cut in 1" circles.

With a spatula move to a lightly oiled cookie sheet.

Bake for 20 minutes at 350°. Let cool before removing from tray.

Yield: 2 doz. cookies

Hearty Oat and Raisin Cookies

Preheat oven to 350°.

1 cup	flour
1 tsp.	baking soda
Dash	sea salt
2 1/4 cups	rolled oats
1/4 cup	wheat germ
3/4 cup	margarine or corn oil
1 cup	brown sugar
2 tsp.	lecithin
1 tsp.	vanilla
1 cup	raisins soaked in water
1/2 cup	chopped walnuts (optional)

Combine all dry ingredients together.

Cream margarine and sugar.

Add dry mixture to the margarine mixture.

Stir in raisins, nuts and 1 cup of liquid from soaked raisins.

Drop by tsp. onto lightly oiled baking sheet.

Flatten lightly by hand.

Bake for 12-15 minutes until brown.

Oatmeal Drop Cookies

Preheat oven to 350°.

Measure and combine:

1/2 cup	honey creamed with
1/2 cup	light vegetable oil

Beat in until smooth

1 tbsp.	liquid lecithin
1 tsp.	pure vanilla
1/4 cup	soy milk

Stir together and add to the above ingredients:

1 cup	whole wheat flour
1 tsp.	no-alum baking powder
1/2 tsp.	sea salt

When smooth add:

1 cup	uncooked rolled oats
1 tbsp.	cocoa or carob powder (optional)

Stir the mixture well.

Drop cookies 2 inches apart on well-oiled cookie sheet.

Bake until light brown, about 15 minutes.

If you let the batter stand for about five minutes before dropping from spoon the oats will make batter thicker.

Anahareo, Dashiel and Django — The Doughnut Eaters.

Chocolate Cherry Volcanos Erupt in Bryant's Cove
(With help From Connie White Crane.)

Preheat oven to 350°.

1 1/2	cups flour
1/3 cup	cocoa (sifted)
1/2 tsp.	baking soda
1/2 tsp.	sea salt
2/3 cup	margarine
1 cup	raw sugar or honey
1 tsp.	lecithin
1 tsp.	vanilla
1/2 tsp.	almond extract
1/4 cup	vinegar
1/4 cup	soy milk
1 1/2 cups	chopped cherries

Sift together flour, baking soda, and sea salt.

Cream margarine and raw sugar, beat in lecithin, vanilla, and almond extract.

Add dry ingredients, alternate with soy milk.

Stir in lightly floured cherries.

Drop by heaping teaspoon onto ungreased cookie sheet.

Form into volcanic peaks.

Bake for 10-12 minutes. Cool and frost with chocolate glaze and top with a cherry. Makes 4 dozen.

Chocolate Glaze

Melt 1/4 cup margarine in saucepan, stir in 1/3 cup cocoa. Blend in 1/4 cup cherry juice, 1/4 tsp. almond extract and 1 cup raw sugar until smooth. Spread over cookies.

Peanut Butter Gems

Preheat oven to 350°.

Beat together until creamy:

1/2 cup	maple syrup
1/2 cup	honey

with

1/2 cup	light oil
1 cup	peanut butter

stir in

1 tsp.	liquid lecithin
1 tsp.	pure vanilla
1/2 tsp.	sea salt

sift, measure and combine with above

2 cups	your combination of flours
2 tsp.	baking powder

(Continued)

Batter should be fairly stiff.

Drop by small amounts onto oiled cookie sheet. Shape in a small ball and press with a fork. Dip fork in water to prevent batter from sticking to it.

Watch them. They cook quickly. Bake for 13 minutes.

Allow to cool before removing from cookie sheet.

Makes 24 cookies.

First Grade Valentine Surprise Cookies

Swiftly stir together:

1/2 cup	corn oil
1 cup	brown sugar
1/2 cup	hot water
1/4 tsp.	almond oil

Sift together

2 cups	durum flour
1 tbsp.	cinnamon
1 tbsp.	no-alum baking powder

Combine liquid and dry ingredients.

Stir until thick and smooth. Add 1/2 cup more flour for extra firm cookies.

Flatten on floured wooden board and shape into hearts with cutter.

Bake at 350° for 20 minutes.

Spread homemade raspberry jelly on cooled cookies.

Maxwell's Tofu Squares

Preheat oven to 350°.

Crust:

1 cup	crunchy granola (no fruit)
2 tsp.	honey
2 tsp.	lemon juice

(Combine and press in pan, reserve 1/4 cup for top)

Puree the following until smooth:

1 1/2 lb.	soft tofu
1/2 cup	pure maple syrup
1/4 cup	minced raisins or minced and pitted dates
4 tbsp.	lemon juice
1/2 tsp.	grated lemon rind
1 tbsp.	tahini
1 tsp.	pure vanilla

Spoon filling over crust and sprinkle with remaining 1/4 cup granola.

Bake for 20 minutes or until surface is lightly brown.

Allow to cool thoroughly (overnight) if you can wait that long!

Greg's Lemon-Pineapple Squares
(one of a kind)

Combine a cup of granola — just grains, no raisins or other fruit — with a handful of rice flour and wheat germ

Cut in

    1/4 cup   light oil and crumble with your hands

Sprinkle spring water over this and press into a 10" x 15" baking pan.

Prick holes in bottom and bake at 350° for 15 minutes.

Meanwhile:

Fill your blender with 5 cups of unsweetened pineapple juice.

Squeeze and add juice of:

    3 lemons   and grated peel of 1

Pour in:

    1/2 cup   honey or maple syrup

While blending add:

    1/2 to 3/4 cup ground almonds and

    7 heaping tbsp.   arrowroot flour (solidifying agent)

Top with:

    1 cup   hot water

Pour into a stainless steel double boiler and heat until thick. Stir constantly. Gradually add another cup of pineapple juice and continue to heat until very thick. Remove crust from oven and pour the sauce over crust (1/8" thick). Place in refrigerator to thoroughly cool. (at least 4 hours).

While Cooling Make This Topping

Cream 1/2 lb. soft tofu with:

    1/2 cup   honey

    1 tbsp.   maple syrup

    1 tsp.   vanilla.

Spread evenly over the lemon squares when they are cool and firm.

Apricot Pudding

Combine:

    5 1/2 cups   water

    1 cup   honey

Bring to a boil over low heat.

Add 1 lb. dried apricots.

Cook for 30 minutes.

Blend the mixture in a food processor.

Return to heat & stir in:

| 1 tbsp. | arrowroot flour |
| 1/2 cup | water |

Bring to a boil & continue to stir for 3 minutes until it is thick.

Spoon into dessert dishes & chill.

Serve with *Soy Cream*

Guilt Ridden Old Fashioned Chocolate Fudge from The Bay

4 tbsp.	grated dark chocolate
1 cup	raw sugar
1 cup	brown sugar
1/8 tsp.	sea salt
1 cup	soy milk
1 tbsp.	margarine
1/2 tsp.	vanilla

Mix together in a saucepan: dark chocolate, raw and brown sugar and sea salt. Add the soy milk and margarine. Bring to a boiling point over medium heat, stirring all the time. Then boil gently until a few drops in cold water forms a soft ball. Remove from heat, add the vanilla.

Place saucepan in cold water, let stand 4 minutes without stirring. Remove from cold water and beat until mixture thickens and loses its glossy appearance (about 5 minutes). Spread in lightly oiled pan ("8 X 8"). When firm cut into small squares.

Doran's Fudge Pudding

1 cup	sifted flour
2 tsp.	baking powder
1/2 tsp.	sea salt
3/4 cup	honey
3 1/2 tbsp.	cocoa or carob
1/2 tbsp.	soy milk
2 tbsp.	margarine
3/4 cup	walnuts (optional)
3/4 cup	brown sugar
1 3/4 cup	hot water.

Sift flour, baking powder, sea salt, honey and 2 tbsp. of the cocoa. Stir together milk, vanilla and oil. Then add dry ingredients and nuts. Pour into 9 inch square pan. Mix brown sugar and remaining cocoa. Sprinkle over batter.

Pour hot water over it all and bake at 350° for 40 minutes.

Welcome Home Blueberry Squares, 1984

Preheat oven to 350°.

1/2 cup	corn meal
1/2 cup	rice flour
1/2 cup	soy flour
1 cup	durum flour
2 tsp.	no alum baking powder
1 tbsp.	cinnamon
1/2 tsp.	nutmeg
1/2 cup	honey
1/2 cup	sunflower oil
3/4 cup	warm spring water
1 1/2 cups	fresh blueberries

Combine first seven ingredients in a stainless steel bowl — then combine the following four.

Mix both together, gently fold in berries last.

Spread into a 8" square baking pan and bake for 30 minutes.

Leave squares in pan while cooling, do not cut until cool unless you want a pudding!

While squares are cooling you can conjure up this sauce. . .

Blend until smooth, then pour over squares and let set in refrigerator for half an hour:

1 cup	melted coconut cream
2 tbsp.	honey
1 tsp.	pure vanilla
1 tbsp.	arrowroot flour

Avondale Blueberry Dash

Preheat oven 350°

In a stainless steel mixing bowl combine:

2 1/2 cups	combination of rice, millet and soy flour
1 tbsp.	no-alum baking powder

In second bowl blend:

1/2 cup	pure maple syrup
1/2 cup	light corn or safflower oil
1/2 cup	warm water or soy milk

Combine the dry ingredients with the second bowl

Fold in 1 cup freshly picked blueberries

Bake 45 minutes in lightly oiled bread pan

While warm, serve with a favourite nut cream

Eldamar Blueberry Blunt

Not unlike a blueberry grunt but made with a little more laissez-faire.
For best results bake in a wood stove.

Cream together:

1 cup	soy milk
1/4 cup	light oil
1/2 cup	honey
3/4 cup	molasses
1 tsp.	egg replacer & 2 tbsp. spring water

Sift in:

2 cups	soft flour, any combination
2 tsp.	no-alum baking powder
1 tsp.	ginger and cinnamon

Line bottom of 5" x 8" pan with 2 cups fresh blueberries and 2 tsp. lemon juice.

Sprinkle with 2 tbsp. arrowroot flour and a dribble of honey

Pour batter over blueberries

Bake for 40 minutes (until berries bubble) at 350°. Serve with *Soy Cream*.

Dock Ridge Partridge Berry Bog

Top of Bog:

1/4 cup	margarine
1/4 tsp.	protein seasoning
1/2 cup	honey
1 tsp.	lecithin
1 tsp.	baking powder
1 cup	soy milk
1 cup	flour
1 tsp.	vanilla

Bottom:

1 cup	apples, sliced thin
1 cup	brown sugar
2 cups	partridge berries
1 tbsp.	arrowroot flour

Cream together margarine, honey, lecithin, and vanilla.

Mix together flour, protein seasoning and baking powder.

Add to the cream mixture alternating with soy milk.

Combine berries & apples and put in a 9 X 9" dish.

Spread 1 tbsp. arrowroot flour over berries and 1 cup brown sugar.

Cover with cream mixture.

Bake at 350° for 40 minutes.

Apple Rhubarb Crisp

Preheat oven to 450°

1 cup	rice flour
1/2 cup	chick pea flour
1/2 cup	soy flour
1/2 cup	raw sugar
1 tsp.	baking soda
1/2 tsp.	Protein Seasoning
10	medium apples
2	rhubarb sprigs

Combine first 6 ingredients and cut in 1/2 cup margarine with a few sprinkles of water.

Layer a large casserole dish with small pieces of diced apple. Mix with 1 cup diced rhubarb. Squeeze the juice of a half lemon over this and 1 cup raw sugar.

Spread and crumble flour mixture over top of casserole. Bake at 425° for 10 minutes and then reduce heat and bake at 350° for 40 minutes.

Serve with fresh *Soy Cream* and a dribble of maple syrup.

Apple Pudding

1/4 cup	margarine
1/2 cup	brown sugar
1 tsp.	egg replacer + 2 tbsp water
1/2 cup	soy milk
1 cup	pastry flour
2 tsp.	baking powder
1/4 tsp.	salt
1/2 tsp.	vanilla

Sauce:

1 cup	brown sugar
1 tbsp.	flour
1 tbsp.	margarine
1/2 tsp.	vanilla
1 1/2 cups	water

Slice apples into an oiled baking dish. Sprinkle with cinnamon. Cream margarine, sugar, egg replacer and vanilla. Then add milk, alternate with sifted dry ingredients. Spread over apples.

Sauce: Combine all ingredients and boil for 5 minutes. Pour over batter, bake for 35-40 minutes at 350°.

Elly Danica's Fresh Pear or Apple Tart

1 tsp.	egg replacer combined with
2 tbsp.	water
1/4 cup	soy milk
1 cup	(or less) raw sugar
Pinch	sea salt
1 tsp.	ginger for pears or
1 tsp.	cinnamon for apples
1 1/2 cups	flour (millet, spelt, or brown rice combination)
2 lbs.	fresh pears or tart apples
1/2 cup	almond or sesame meal

Preheat oven to 375°.

Beat egg substitute, water and milk together in a bowl. Add sugar and sea salt, and continue to beat. Add flour, mixing it thoroughly to produce a smooth batter.

Peel pears or apples, cut them lengthwise into quarters, then cut across in slices. Add to batter in bowl.

Smear a 9" round spring foam cake pan with oil, sprinkle lightly with crumbs or meal. Turn pan over and give it a sharp rap over sink to loosen excess crumbs.

Put batter in pan, level off with back of a spoon or spatula. Dribble a little oil over tart. Bake for approximately 50 minutes, or until top has become a light golden brown.

When cake is done, but still warm, loosen from pan and transfer to platter.

This tart has an almost pudding like texture.

Good served with a chocolate, raspberry coulis or any favourite sweet sauce or unaccompanied while warm.

Non-Traditional Strawberry Shortcake

(Yield: 10 individual shortcakes)

Filling:

3 cups	fresh strawberries
1/2 cup	honey

Biscuit Dough:

2 cups	light flour
1 tbsp.	baking powder
1/2 tsp.	sea salt
1/2 cup	non-hydrogenated margarine
3/4 cup	soy milk
2 tbsp.	raw sugar
1 tsp.	pure vanilla

Topping:

    1 1/3 cups   prepared *Soy Cream*

Rinse and hull your local strawberries.

Preserve 6 whole berries for garnish and mash remainder.

Place mashed berries in medium bowl and sprinkle 1/2 cup raw sugar over top.

Set aside until serving time.

In a large bowl, sift together flour, baking powder, sea salt and sugar.

Cut in margarine until mixture resembles fine crumbs.

Slowly add soy milk and mix until flour is evenly moistened. Do not over mix.

Drop by heaping tablespoonfuls (2" apart) on an oiled cookie sheet.

Bake at 425° for 12-14 minutes or until golden brown.

Prepare *Soy Cream*.

Method: Slice shortcake in half horizontally. Remove top. Place one cake layer on round serving platter, cut-side up. Spoon on mashed berries.

Place second layer over berries and top with soy cream.

Garnish with whole berries and serve warm.

Christmas Pudding Bubbles Brown

Have ready a large pot of boiling water.

Hand blend well:

1 cup	honey
1/2 cup	sunflower oil

Add:

1 cup	soy milk
1 cup	mild flavoured molasses
2 tsp.	liquid lecithin
1 cup	seedless raisins
1 cup	chopped figs

Sift together:

5 cups	unbleached white and soft whole wheat flour
1 tbsp.	cinnamon
1 tsp.	ginger, nutmeg and cloves (each)
2 tsp.	no-alum baking powder

Add sifted ingredients to the molasses mixture.

Pour batter into a well-oiled pudding mold, 3/4" full.

Steam for 1 1/2 hours.

Important: once removed from pot, remove lid or pudding will get soggy as it cools.

Serve hot with *Lemon-Orange Cody* (next page).

Lemon Orange Cody:

Simmer till hot

	juice of 2 lemons
	juice of 1 lime
	juice of 3 oranges
1 cup	maple syrup

If you prefer a thicker sauce add 2 tbsp. arrowroot flour to juice of one orange. Gradually stir into remainder of sauce.

Irie Christmas Fruit Cake, 1980.

(A good year to make cakes. My friend, Doran, and I made 30! Like Elves at 5 a.m. we rescued the last four from the oven.)

In a bowl mix the following dry ingredients:

3 1/2 cups	soft whole wheat sifted flour or other *irie* combination of flour.
1 tsp.	baking powder
1 tsp.	baking soda
3 tsp.	cinnamon
2 tsp.	allspice
1/2 tsp.	nutmeg
1/4 tsp.	ground cloves
1 tsp.	sea salt or salt substitute

In a large mixing bowl or blender make a buttery mixture from:

3 cups	*Nut Milk*
3/4 cup	pure maple syrup
3/4 cup	light unrefined vegetable oil
1 tbsp.	lecithin

You'll need to combine the following in a third bowl:

1/2 cup	chopped walnuts
1/2 cup	chopped almonds
1/2 cup	chopped pecans
1 cup	raisins
1 cup	currants
1 cup	chopped dried apricots
	Grated peel of 1 orange
	Grated peel of 1 lime (retain juice)

Mix and dust with a handful of flour

Pour juice over the above.

Combine the fruit and nut mixture with the buttery mixture.

Gradually beat in the spiced flour.

Preheat oven to 250°.

Prepare a cast iron pot with well-oiled brown paper cut to fit the bottom.

Pour in batter, smoothing the top.

Bake for 3 hours.

Insert a straw in the centre to determine if it has cooked all the way to the bottom. If any cake sticks to straw, bake for an extra half hour.

Carrot Cake

Preheat oven to 350°

3 1/2 cups	unsifted combination of light flours
2 tsp.	no-alum baking powder
1 tsp.	sea salt
2 tsp.	cinnamon
1 tsp.	powdered cloves
1 cup	honey
1 cup	mild flavoured molasses
1/2 cup	sunflower oil
2 tsp.	liquid lecithin
2 cups	finely grated carrot
1/2 cup	chopped dates or
1/2 cup	crushed and strained pineapple
1 cup	chopped walnuts (optional)

In one bowl combine molasses, honey, oil, lecithin, grated carrots, dates and walnuts.

In another stir together measured flour, spices and baking powder.

Gradually add dry ingredients to the liquid combination to form a stiff mixture.

Pour into a well-oiled baking pan and bake for 45 minutes. Remove from pan and cool on a cooling rack.

Grandmother Hall's Apple Cake Extrodinaire

1 1/4 cups	flour
1/2 cup	brown sugar
1/4 tsp.	salt
1 tsp.	cinnamon
2 cups	chopped apples
1 cup	raisins
1/2 cup	chopped walnuts
1 tsp.	egg replacer + 2 tbsp. water
1/2 cup	orange juice
1 tsp.	baking soda
1/2 cup	oil
1 tsp.	vanilla

Combine dry ingredients.

Combine apples, raisins, nuts, orange juice, oil and vanilla.

Add dry ingredients to apple mixture.

Pour into oiled 8" square pan.

Bake at 350° for 45 to 50 minutes.

Ginger-Pineapple Bake

Blend:

1/2 cup	maple syrup
1 cup	fresh pineapple (or in a pinch use unsweetened canned pineapple).

In a bowl mix thoroughly and then add to blended mixture:

1 1/2 cups	whole wheat pastry flour or other combination of flours
1 tsp.	ginger
1 tsp.	cinnamon
1/2 tsp.	allspice
1/2 tsp.	ground cloves
1 tbsp.	no-alum baking powder

Bake at 350° for 25-30 minutes

Top with *Soy Cream* before serving.

Anahareo's Raisin-Nut Birthday Cake

Preheat oven to 350°

Whiz in a blender:

1 cup	warm soy milk
1 cup	honey or maple syrup
1 tsp.	pure vanilla
1 tsp.	grated lemon rind
1/2 tsp.	ground anise seed or oil of anise
1/2 cup	sunflower oil
1 tsp.	protein seasoning

Sift together:

2 1/2 cups	unbleached white flour

Add:

1 1/2 tsp.	baking powder
1/4 cup	wheat germ

Combine blended mixture with dry ingredients.

Add:

1 cup	raisins (soaked and drained).
1/4 cup	walnuts or pecans (chopped)

Prepare two cake pans by oiling and sprinkling flour on the bottom and sides of the pans. Pour batter to half their depth.

Bake for 35 – 40 minutes. Let cool thoroughly before spreading top with carob icing or coconut topping.

For carob icing see *Extra-Terrestrial Raised Doughnut* recipe, page 20.

To make *Coconut Topping* simply melt 1 block of pure concentrated coconut with just enough water to keep coconut from sticking. Sweeten with 1/4 cup maple syrup.

Watermelon Drink

Remove rind from melon

Blend the red pulp together with seeds for 2 minutes.*

Strain the liquid for a smooth, refreshing drink.

*Seeds aid in the digestion of the watermelon

Vanilla Shakes A Winters Night in 1987

2 cups	soy milk
1 tbsp.	pure vanilla
3 tbsp.	malt liquid or powder
3 tbsp.	pure maple syrup

Blend in 1 banana, 6-8 strawberries, or your favourite fruit.

Add a little ice while blending and serve immediately.

Lavender Shake

2 cups	soy milk
1 cup	blueberries
1/8 cup	maple syrup
1	banana
4	ice cubes

Blend until smooth.

Serve chilled.

Carob Milkshake

1	banana
1 tsp.	carob
2 cups	almond *Nut Milk*
1 tbsp.	maple syrup

Blend until smooth. Serve immediately.

Nut Milk

Note: Soak nuts and/or seeds (almond, sesame or sunflower) for two hours.

Soak 1 1/2 cups nuts or seeds in 1 qt of spring water.

Blend with soak water until creamy (2 to 3 minutes.)

Add: 1 tbsp. lecihtin.

For a thinner milk continue to add water. Strain off excess pulp.

For a sweet milk add 1 tbsp. of maple syrup.

Soy Cream

Blend:

3/4 cup	soy milk with
1 cup	light oil, continue adding oil until a thick cream forms (could take up to 2 cups)

Add:

1/4 cup	maple syrup
1 tsp.	vanilla
1 tsp.	lemon juice

Chill and spoon over dessert.

Banana Ice Cream

Peel 4 well-ripened bananas.

Place in an air tight plastic bag (stick a straw in the corner of the bag & suck out additional air) before sealing bag.

Place in freezer for at least 8 hours.

Remove from freezer bags & push each banana through a champion juicer into cone. Not unlike a custard cone.

Serve as is or dipped in a carob or chocolate sauce.

Vegetable Cocktail Party

Almost any combination of vegetables can be juiced together or used separately. Wash vegetables thoroughly before juicing.

Juice:

6	medium carrots
1	beet
2 stalks	celery
2	apples (cored)

Strain well before serving. Remember that digestion begins in the mouth, so chew your juice and drink your food!

Glossary

Broth and Seasoning: There are many packaged vegetable broths on the market today, but I always prefer this organic broth and seasoning put out by Dr. Bernard Jensen.

Coffee Substitute: A beverage served hot and made from chicory, barley, and other grains. If you don't expect the sharp taste of coffee or the buzz, you won't be disappointed.

CuisineArt: A multi faceted electric food processor that makes food preparing a lot easier.

Gluten: This product is derived from the kneading of flour and water to remove the starch. (see Barbecue Gluten recipe for further details.)

Lecithin: a soy derivative that acts as an emulsifying agent. Use in place of an egg. (1 tsp. = 1 egg)

No aluminium baking powder: The same as regular baking powder except that it has the aluminum by-product removed in the processing.

Nutritional Yeast Flakes: Not to be confused with dry, active yeast. Nutritional yeast is yet another derivative of the soy bean. It is made from the husk of the bean and is said to be high in B-12. However if you have concerns about allergies it is best to avoid all yeast products. Keep in a dark jar to prevent light from destroying the B - vitamin.

Protein Seasoning: One of the tastiest Bernard Jensen products. Made from ground vegetables, it is also high in sodium, so there is certainly no need to use additional salt when using this product. Keep in freezer to prevent from lumping together.

Rice Dream: An alternative to ice cream that I don't make but I enjoy immensely. It is one of the healthiest deserts since it is made almost entirely from rice!

Sauté: Lightly fry.

Soy Cheese: A tofu soy product. Strict vegetarians beware, soy cheese most often contains casein, an animal derivative as a firming agent.

T.V.P.: Texturized Vegetable Protein. An inexpensive food derived from soy bean pulp. Can be make by grinding soaked soy beans and drying in the oven for 40 minutes at 350°. Available at most health food stores.

Tahini: This is a smooth spread made form fresh ground sesame seeds. When unrefined it is rich in calcium. Tahini can be used in a variety of sauces, as well as a spread for bread and pancakes.

Tempeh: A refined product made by fermenting soy beans. Can be used in a variety of dishes from a vegetable stir fry to vegie burgers.

Vegetable Broth: A quick and tasty broth made by adding 1 tbsp. Bernard Jensen broth and seasoning to 1 cup hot water. You can also purchase B.J. Mineral Bouillon.

Wheatlets: Not unlike gluten. This product made from flour is now being shaped into every imaginable meatless product from tofu wieners to chicken nuggets.

Recommended Reading for a Wholistic Approach to Health:

The Real Soup and Salad Book by Dr. Bernard Jensen

The Tofu Cookbook by Louise Hagler

The Farm Vegetarian Cookbook by Hagler & Bates

Survival Into The Twenty-First Century by Victoras Kulvinskas

(The New) Healing Yourself by Joy Gardner

Our Earth Our Cure by Raymond Dextreit

School of Natural Healing by Dr. John Christopher

Index

SOUPS:
Beet Soup, 6
Borsch, 5
Corn Chowder, 7
Gazpacho, 5
I-tal Soup, 7
Lentil Soup, 4
Lima Bean Soup, 3
Minestrone, 5
Miso Bean Soup, 3
Soup a l'Ongnon, 6
Split Pea Soup, 4
Tofu Soup, 7
Zucchini Soup, 4

SALADS:
Bean Salad, 11
Caesar Salad, 9
Cole Slaw, 10
Fruit Salad, 9
Garden Salad, 9
Potato Salad
    (Summer), 11
Potato Salad
    (Newfanese), 11
Sprout Salads, 10

SALAD DRESSINGS:
Colour Therapy
    Dressing, 12
Guacamole, 15
Parsley Garlic
    Dressing, 13
Pesto, 13
Soyanaise Dressing, 12
Rejuvelac, 14
Tahini Dressing, 12
Tofu Dressing, 13
Tossed Salad
    Dressing, 13
Yogurt, 14
Winter's Breakfast, 15

**BREADS, PASTRIES &
PANCAKES:**
Apple Pie, 33
Banana Bread, 23
Blueberry Pie, 34
Bran Muffins, 27
Corn Meal Buns, 26
Cinnamon Rolls, 19
Crepes, Heavenly, 31
Creps, Savory, 31
Doughnuts, 20
Figgy Duff, 24
Ginger Bread, 23
Honey Scones, 27
Lassy Bread, 22
Pancakes, Special, 29
Pancakes (Apple), 30

Pancakes (Diet), 31
Pancakes (Scorpio), 30
Pie Crust, 32
Pita Bread, 25
Pumpernickel Bread, 22
Pumpkin Pie, 32
Raspberry Tofu "Cheese-
    cake" Pie, 33
Soup Biscuits, 28
Tea Buns (Figgie
    Lizzie), 26
Tofu Herb Rolls, 25
Turnovers (Raspberry), 32
Wheat Germ Muffins, 28
Whole Wheat Protein
    Bread, 21
Zucchini Loaf, 29

MAIN DISHES:
Baked Beans, 54
Baked Brown Rice, 42
Cabbage Rolls, 51
Chick-Pea Festive
    Loaf, 48
Chili Sans Carne, 53
Chips (No Fuss), 59
Choux-flours
    au Gratin, 41
Dandelion Scoff, 57
Devilled Eggless
    Sandwiches, 62
Eggplant, 45
Enchiladas, 39
Fettucini, 56
Ginger Stir Fry, 53
Gluten, Festive Barbecue,
    50
Gravy (Pagan Vegan), 59
Lasagna (Tofu style), 44
Millet Pie, 49
Moussaka, 45
Pesto, 60
Pot Pie, 52
Potato Dip, 62
Quiche, Tofu &
    Spinach, 57
Quick Summer Meal, 42
Relish (Piccalli), 60
Relish (Sweet), 60
Rice (Baked Brown), 42
Rice Dumplings, 61
Salsa, 62
Scallop (Gluten) Casse-
    role, 56
Scalloped Potatoes, 42
Shepardless Pie, 46
Soka, 61
Soy Loaf, 47
Spanokapita a la
    Sandrosco, 47

Stew (Wild
    Chanterelle), 48
Stuffing, 59
Tacky Taco, 39
Tempeh Casserole, 40
Tofu Burgers, 38
Tofu Coating, 61
Vegetable Curry, 58
Veggie Burgers, 38
Vegie Pate a Lorraine, 43
Yeast Sauce, 46
Zucchini (Stuffed), 54

DESSERTS:
Apple Cake, 77
Apple Rhubarb Crisp, 73
Apple Pudding, 73
Apple Tart, 74
Apricot Pudding, 69
Banana Ice Cream, 80
Blueberry Blunt, 72
Blueberry Dash, 71
Blueberry Pudding, 71
Blueberry Squares, 71
Carob Milkshake, 79
Carrot Cake, 77
Chocolate Cherry
    Volcanos, 67
Chocolate Fudge, 70
Christmas Fruit Cake, 76
Christmas Pudding, 75
Fudge Pudding, 70
Ginger Delights, 65
Ginger-Pineapple Bake, 78
Lavendar Shake, 79
Lemon-Pineapple
    Squares, 69
Nut Milk, 80
Oat & Raisin
    Cookies, 65
Oatmeal Drop
    Cookies, 66
Partridge Berry Bog, 72
Peanut Butter Gems, 67
Pear Tart, 74
Raisin-nut Birthday Cake,
    78
Soy Cream, 80
Strawberry Shortcake, 74
Tofu Squares, 68
Valentine Surprise
    Cookies, 68
Vanilla Shakes, 79
Vegetable Cocktail
    Drink, 80
Watermelon Drink, 79